VLADIMIR BERZONSKY

The Gift of Love

ST VLADIMIR'S SEMINARY PRESS
CRESTWOOD, NEW YORK 10707
1985

Library of Congress Cataloging in Publication Data

Berzonsky, Vladimir, 1936-
The gift of love.

1. Love—Religious aspects—Christianity—Meditations.
2. Bible. O.T. Song of Solomon—Meditations.
3. Bible. N.T. Corinthians, 1st, XIII—Meditations.
4. Spiritual life—Orthodox Eastern authors. I. Title.
BV4639.B465 1985 241'.4 85-19655
ISBN 0-88141-041-1

THE GIFT OF LOVE

ISBN 0-88141-041-1

PRINTED IN THE UNITED STATES OF AMERICA
BY
ATHENS PRINTING COMPANY
New York, NY 10018

THE GIFT OF LOVE

To all who taught me Love.

Table of Contents

Preface

Love is a gift from God, a sacred grace that invites us, indeed challenges us to respond with whatever capability we have within us to love God, one another, and His creation. All of the chapters in this book were written and intended to be read separately; yet, they all deal with the constant theme of love as expressed in the Bible.

Much has been written in the recent past regarding the difference between erotic love and the selfless, outpouring love that is agape, which is both Christ-like and Christian; but it is the former type of love that conditions us for the latter. We learn to love in stages, developing an ever greater power to become godlike in our affections, increasing our capacity to care less for self and become filled with concern for God and all He made.

Here is why the Song of Songs sets forth the theme. It is an erotic poem when read on the obvious level, expressing the yearnings of a man and woman for one another; however, at deeper levels of understanding, the lyrics of love far supersede mere sexual emotions, revealing the divine outpouring of affection of God for His handiwork, and also revealing creation's response.

Love is a mystery revealed in Christ Jesus. Were it not for Him, we would be reduced to our own paltry, all-too-human knowledge of love, limited by our creatureliness to expressions such as Rozanov expressed, feeling he was uttering a profound, complete definition by equating love with the air we breathe:

> "To love"—means "I cannot do without you; I am depressed without you; it is dull wherever you are not present." This is an external, but a most precise description of love. Love is not fire (as is often stated), love is air. Without it, there is no breath, and with it—one breathes easily. (V. Rozanov, *Opavshiya Listya* [Fallen Leaves], 1915, p. 8.)

Love as air, as the source of the life we now live, is yet not enough, since it expresses only our creaturely love. God's love, one that will take upon itself our fleshly state, condescending to live, to age, to realize our pain, our anguish, our emotions, our fear of dying and even death itself, all because He loved us enough to lead us through it all—that inconceivable, overwhelming love we humans can only begin to conceptualize.

I. FROM SOLOMON'S SONG OF SONGS

1
Holy Kisses

O that you would kiss me with the kisses of your mouth!
(Song of Songs 1:2)

At first we are startled, taken aback at the passionate imagery of this book from the sacred scriptures. This is the very Bible, containing the word of the Lord. We identify it with the Church. We expect it to be more aloof, reserved, even imperial, since for us who were raised in a formal Church, such majesty would be most fitting. Almost embarrassingly out of place appears this bold desire for a passionate kiss, an intimacy more appropriate to a novel, or an afternoon television soap opera.

Yet the Church has a great deal of kissing among believers. "Greet one another with a holy kiss," St Paul recommends. And who would celebrate the joy of Pascha without exchanging kisses? Orthodox priests always kiss one another during the Divine Liturgy.

The most apparent meaning of a kiss is a response to love. Here is the sense of the phrase under study. It cries out for some overt reaction to the great love that overwhelms the one who is speaking. It asks for more than merely a single kiss, but a great number of them, to demonstrate the intensity of love which is calling for a reaction. Since here the Lord Almighty is the Speaker, we feel how dismally inadequate is the idea that we may have of a God somewhere beyond us, far away from the world and ourselves. The very God who made us has a passionate longing for His creatures to love Him in response. That reality is affirmed in numerous writings of the fathers who lived in the desert, depriving themselves of all worldly pleasures in order to make themselves ready to receive the love of God poured out upon His saints.

A single kiss can be accidental or merely ceremonial. Now that our society is losing touch with its deepest emotions, a handshake is frequently felt inadequate as a sign of greeting. People often kiss upon meeting, but in a perfunctory, unemotional way that is as vapid as a flabby handshake. They touch cheeks ever so lightly, or kiss without really kissing, probably to avoid suggesting a deeper intimacy. But in the Song of Songs, the Lover pleads for an outpouring of kisses. One might say that Eastern Christians exchange three "holy" kisses to show they mean to demonstrate affection, since one might be accidental and two yearn for completion, but three times make the action indelible.

And the demand is for kisses on the lips. Not pallid pecks on the cheek, but a hearty response to God's outcry for love. This is how God truly loves us, the text is singing out, and this is the way He expects us to reciprocate. He made us capable of loving Him affectionately, and He desires that we do so.

Watch a mother as she washes and dresses her newborn child. Does she ever do just the necessary, or will she not play with the infant, taking delight in its touch, cooing to it, and kissing it many times over? When would a bystander tell her it's enough, and why would anybody want to bring her pure affection to a halt? So beautiful, and so fitting. Yet God loves us even more than the most loving of mothers. Yes, difficult to imagine, perhaps, but this is true simply because God has an infinite capacity to love. The mother loves what she has brought into the world; God loves what He created.

Put another way, Jesus Christ is telling us the good news that God desires to have a love affair with the world. But His love too often goes unrequited. The world chooses to love itself, not its Maker. The people the Lord created with the capacity to return His love limit themselves to lusting after what He created, which will not last and which is unworthy of them. Forsaking the Creator, they serve idols: wealth, security, diplomas, medals, symbols of success, security, or worldly acclaim. They do not spend their lives learning the means of returning to God the affection He desires. God's kisses fall on humanity's cold lips.

2
Leaves of Love

Your name is like perfume poured out;
no wonder the maidens love you!
(Song of Songs 1:3)

Presently our world's ways of communicating are undergoing a radical transformation, and computers are taking the lead in the process. Society is absorbed, intrigued, and obsessed with the instrument. Predictions are for uncounted uses not yet imagined; nevertheless, there is one kind of communication that computers cannot be programmed to help us transmit, our discourse with Almighty God. For that we require the Holy Bible, sacred worship, and our prayer books.

What a treasure is a battered old prayer book. How precious are they, used daily and over many years. The spines have long since been broken; the leaves are browned and smudged from uncounted handlings; the lower corners are rounded or broken off. Some pages have separated from the binding and no longer line up neatly with their mates. Faded ribbons or paper icons of the sort left at homes during the epiphany blessings or distributed by funeral homes sometimes divide morning from evening prayers. But the booklets themselves are evidence of the devotion of their owners. In a sense, they might be considered passports to the Kingdom of Heaven.

The owner of such a prayer book died recently. I wondered what her family would do with that sign of her communication with the Lord. It's not the sort of item one includes in a will. Probably it will remain among the photos and keepsakes stuffed into an envelope and tucked away in a drawer somewhere, forgotten forever. That is, if a relative does not get the notion to place it into the coffin. Not everybody has a use for a used prayer book. Not in these times.

I recall once visiting an elderly woman in a nursing home. The beds were arranged in dormitory fashion, six or eight ladies to a room. Immediately upon entering I became the focus of attention, an oddity to stare at on an otherwise conventionally dull afternoon. My problem soon became how to conduct the private confession in so public a setting, with a person who, it soon became evident, was stone deaf, and in the midst of attentive, curious onlookers. First I used a stage whisper in English, then cleared my throat and tried a bit louder, this time in Russian, presuming nobody but the two of us could speak in so foreign a language. No response proceeded from my would-be confessee. Rather, she stared at me in puzzlement and would punctuate my pitiful phrases with intermittent squeals of "Eh?"

As I paused to regroup my inner resources, my eyes fell upon that cherished sign of the one thing needful in life, the familiar prayer book so aptly titled "Soul Bread." There it was, half hidden in the ample folds of her smock, properly tattered and faded from much use.

Did it really matter that she was not able to respond to the strangely frustrated young priest who visited her that afternoon? It was abundantly evident that she had little problem communicating with her true Source of nourishment and comfort. What need had she to converse with me, or for that matter, with the company of strangers with whom she was forced to spend the remaining days of her life on this earth, as long as she was in touch with the One who invites her to abide with Him like a branch of a tree joined to its trunk?

I find myself looking for those worn prayer books whenever

I meet somebody for the first time, for I have long held the notion that one is able to discern something of a person by discovering what he enjoys reading.

3
The Desire for Christ

My lover is to me a sachet of myrrh
resting between my breasts.
(Song of Songs 1:13)

Ask Christians what baptism is about and the answer will nearly always contain the understanding of purification from sins, spiritual cleansing, and perhaps exorcism and the start of a new life. All that is, of course, precisely correct; yet, something else takes place besides the immersion. In fact, another sacrament occurs—the anointing with Holy Chrism.

Perhaps many who are present at baptisms are not even aware of the Chrismation, intrigued as they are by the drama surrounding the immersion and its effects: Is the baby crying? Was the water not too cold? Will the child catch cold? And all the while, the priest is making invisible little crosses at each of the orifices of the newly baptized's head, as well as on his breast and back, hands and feet. This is a gift intended to instill ardor into the person, a burning love for Jesus Christ that will influence every act and thought of his lifetime.

We recall that myrrh was one of the costly gifts of the Magi at the birth of Jesus in Bethlehem. As gold gave tribute to His kingly stature and frankincense signified His priestly function for our salvation, so myrrh revealed that He would die on our behalf, which was the key element in God's plan for humanity's redemption. The apostles recollected the scene during that last week of His life on earth, when the woman entered as they were dining and broke an expensive bottle of myrrh, anointing His feet with it as the fragrance permeated the entire house. The same love she manifested for Him must be ours as well, if we begin to comprehend the meaning of the Father's plan for our unity with Him in Christ, guided by the Holy Spirit.

First we must come to learn what God did for us in Christ by reading the Bible and sharing in the remembrance of His workings throughout history as recalled and recreated in the sacred worship of the Church. But learning is not complete without a loving union with the One whose actions we grow to comprehend at ever deeper levels of understanding through a lifetime of study and meditation. The Church does not hesitate to use the language of love to illuminate that sacred, mystical desire to be with Christ, a desire that inspires and motivates all true believers whether awake or sleeping, in every circumstance of life. That desire will suffer many challenges throughout a lifetime. Idolatry, which the Bible puts in first place among sins, manifests itself in varied and subtle ways. Whatever comes between Christ's love for us and our love for Him, no matter how noble or significant, falls within that category. This includes the close relationship we form with other human beings.

As we continue in our repentance and prayers, the fragrance of Christ will draw us forward through the world into the Kingdom of the Father, for the desire to be with Christ includes our response to the invitation of the Holy Trinity to a union planned for humanity. This is what the fathers of the Church describe when they theologize. St Symeon the New Theologian is filled with such exclamations of mystical love, as can be seen in the following example.

> Your beauty is extraordinary, Your appearance without comparison, Your magnificence is inexpressible, Your glory is beyond human language . . . And for this

reason the desire and love that draw us to You conquer over every other love and desire of mortals.

(Hymn 39)

4
The Invitation

Arise, my love, my fair one, and come away;
for lo, the winter is past, the rain is over and gone.
The flowers appear on the earth, the time
of singing has come . . .
(Song of Songs 2:10)

Could there be more welcome words than these, especially when they are spoken by the Lord? If we might dare imagine what our Savior Jesus Christ announced to Adam, Eve, and all those He released from the dark imprisonment of death as depicted on the holy icon of the Resurrection, could it not have been these sounds of joy and release in the song of love between God and humanity? If a flag were to fly over our Christian cemeteries, these words might serve as a motto: "Arise, my love."

Yes, arise from that last bed in the earth, because He did not create us to rest eternally in the earth, but to be with Him where He dwells, in a place where death has neither meaning nor existence. "My love" He calls us. Arise because you are loved by the only true Lover who matters. And we, limited by our creatureliness, living for the most part in the dark forest of the world among spiritual dwarfs, fall asleep like Snow White, to be awakened by a kiss from the unique Prince of life everlasting.

He calls us beautiful, but His vision of what is "fair" has

little to do with the measurements of a Miss America. Hands chapped and calloused from toil for others are lovelier to Him than those with long, lacquered fingernails, and eyes that have looked with kindness and tenderness on others need no eye shadow to hold His gaze. Better are the muscles in the arms and back earned from honest work than body tone made out of self-indulgence.

How wonderful that we need not wait until we are near death to accept this invitation to arise and come away. When we discover true prayer, we learn the uplifting transport that raises us from the sinking, oppressive heaviness of separation from the Lord. The alienation this world insists on is the mark of maturity and individuality, which is instead the result of pride and blindness. How wrong-headed it is to presume that we can be whole persons without having the Spirit of God within us and the awareness of unity with the Father through the Son who desires to make us His siblings.

"Come away . . .," a phrase of arresting power, as realized by advertising experts to sell air flights, beverages, and cigarettes by suggesting that their products' use will provide an experience above the mundane. Falsehoods inflated by the power of suggestion, they are so unlike the power of God that breaks into our fleeting time to grasp us on our way to death and raises us to realize the joy of living in His Kingdom while we are yet on earth.

They are wrong who would term this a form of escape, for Christ Himself, knowing the joy of life in the Kingdom, "emptied himself, taking the form of a servant" (Ph 2:6), as a measure and example not to seek flight from the world, but to reach for an ever fuller experience of the transport that comes through God's love, to wear ourselves out in striving for ways to share the faith and knowledge given to us by Him with those with whom we share this space and time.

5
The Ultimate Love Story

When I found him whom my soul loves,
I held him and would not let him go . . .
(Song of Songs 3:4)

Something is special, unique about the other with whom we are in love. As in the poem "Bonnie Lesley" by Robert Burns:

> To see her is to love her and love but her forever,
> For nature made her what she is and never made another.

When the Church upholds the doctrine of the everlasting virginity of the Mother of our Lord God and Savior, Jesus Christ, not only is She affirming the understanding of the Bible to which Christians have held fast since the earliest days of the Church. A fundamental truth about true love is also revealed by this dogma, one not always evident to many who share these times with us: true love is not interchangeable. It is, on the contrary, once-for-all and forever.

Not only the Church, but any society determined to produce and to protect sound, stable families insists that one man marry one woman and remain with her forever. It realizes that children will grow up healthier and mentally more stable when they have not only "a" father and "a" mother, but also the same parents to nurture and to love them always. Neither parents nor lovers are randomly appointed. Some societies, such as the one in which we now live, pretend that such can be the case.

An irony of our society is that while our culture is so infatuated with romance, by making it a game of changing partners it either has forgotten or chosen to ignore the most rudimentary principle of love, which is uniqueness; thus, it reduces love to merely physical relationships. Shakespeare could never have written the profound "Romeo and Juliet" in these times, because the passion that motivates the lovers, compelling them to be united with one another regardless of social, political, or familial impediments, was a love that transcended mere sensuality. For them it was imperative that they be joined together in the sight of God in holy matrimony. They had to be married, only to one another, and forever. The concept of their union against all who would thwart or prevent their love, a love that ultimately not even death could subdue, makes of the drama a comedy to those who understand love, but a tragedy to those who do not comprehend the unique aspect of their affection.

For those in the Church the Virgin Mary embodies the same once-forever nature of love. She of all maidens on earth was chosen in a mystical manner to become God's "bride." Not only from among all the Hebrew girls, or from all the young women alive at the time God chose to send His unique Son to save the world from sin, but from all who have ever or shall ever live. Actually, the world since Adam and Eve's time was being prepared for this "marriage," so to speak, when God would select a woman from a people He had nurtured for that moment of union between Creator and what He had created, between the Eternal and the dying. Nothing like it had ever been, or will ever be. Here is the supreme, sublime "love story."

Every Christian marriage is a type of that unique love, emulating that aspect of selection for all eternity, a joining forever of a pair of lovers to live for and to love only one another, affirming their union against any and all who would separate them. They are not interchangeable or transferable, despite what this world considers to be love. True love is always and at all times reserved for one man and one woman exclusively.

6
Marriage: Reigning with Love

Behold King Solomon, with the crown with which his mother crowned him on the day of his wedding, on the day of the gladness of his heart.
(Song of Songs 3:11)

"But why would you not wish to wear crowns at the holy mystery of matrimony?" the priest asked the young couple, but he understood the reason which they could not articulate. They are products of a culture that has low aspirations for a family. Marriage is not a vocation for those moderns today who have no concept of mastering life. It is enough for them merely to cope. Still, the Church insists that a bride and groom be queen and king, reigning over their province and taking responsibility for all that is entrusted to their care. The crowns are symbols of rule, but they suggest more than the governance of oneself or one's children.

After the peace ushered in by St Constantine the Great, the Church came to use crowns at weddings as the sign of victory over lusts. As one Church father wrote,

> Crowns are put on their heads as a sign that they never yielded and now come to marriage because they were not overcome by lusts.

Directly following the crowning act, the celebrant lifts

high the holy cross above the heads of the marriage pair and calls upon God to "crown them with honor and glory." He later prays for them to have an "honorable marriage, and an undefiled bed."

Virginity has been and still remains the standard for the unmarried who call themselves Christians. No gift can a person in love offer to the one whom he or she is about to wed that is more precious than one's own body pure, virginal, and undefiled. The mores of a loose society notwithstanding, this truth remains the norm and expectation of the Christian Church.

Guilt is experienced directly following the surrender of a fundamental principle, especially one's virginity, which is written on the heart of each person created in the image of God. Some scholars feel that the Adam and Eve story is really about sexuality told in a more acceptable form, the eating of fruit. Blame comes from within. To accuse the Church of causing people to feel guilty about sex is both wrong and misleading. Not the Church, but something deep within the person tells him or her when he/she is in sin. As the Lord asked Adam hiding in the bushes: "Who told you you were naked?" It is that awareness that we were made to be united with God that reminds us that we have fallen away from Him. The mission of the Church is to continue the forgiveness inaugurated by Jesus Christ. Surely it cannot be that we shall find inner peace when we deny that the guilt exists or that a sin had been committed. That is of no help at all. Christ through the Church forgives sins, but only when we acknowledge that we have erred, blaming nobody but ourselves, undergoing a complete transformation of heart and mind with a pledge to "sin no more."

There is no such thing as free love. Something so precious always comes with a price, and society has no right to pretend to offer what it neither possesses nor controls. Forgiveness does not come by enlightenment, which sometimes our society offers the guilty. Only Jesus Christ is in a position to forgive, since He paid with total obedience, even to death, the admission price to salvation for all who follow and trust in Him. Christ makes us free, but in order to be like Him one must be free from sin, wholesome and pure within and without. Not society, not others, but something deep within each of us lets us know when we are true or false to our real selves. We can never really be hypocrites to our consciences.

7
From Women's Eyes

You have ravished my heart, my sister, my bride, you have ravished my heart with a glance of your eyes.
(Song of Songs 4:9)

Throughout the land of the former Russia, which now in this century is the Soviet Union, decades of atheistic communism notwithstanding, one significant symbol remains—the woman responding to the events of history. When the country was called Holy Russia she was the omnipresent Theotokos, the Birth-giver of God and ever virgin Mary. She remains there today, a silent witness to all that has transpired.

Even the Soviets, despite their renunciation of the nation's Christian past and their defiant atheism, have evidently no other means to depict sorrow and grief than in the faces of women. Throughout the land there are monuments to what Americans call World War II, but which they term the "Great Patriotic War." In nearly every scene where the agony of warfare is depicted, it issues from a woman's sad countenance in stone, wood, or metal.

What is strikingly self-evident, even more so for a people who are able to comprehend nonverbal messages, the post-revolutionary female figures have nothing redemptive in their faces, no sign of hope that can bring a meaning even to suffering, the sign that the blessed Theotokos conveys through all of her icons.

The famous Vladimir icon, for example, depicts in a sublimely sensitive manner the tension between the human, natural love that a mother has for her first-born son, something that not only a woman but any living creature can understand, and the awareness that this special child will become a sacrificial offering for the entire world. Not to have known what was to transpire was not her privilege, for she was informed by the prophet Simeon about what would take place. But her sorrow was tempered by an overriding trust in the God whose ways surpassed human comprehension. Thus, there is sorrow, but not despair. In her face we discover humanity's salvation. And we find reflected in our hearts the courage to go on regardless of what appears to our limited minds to be incomprehensible suffering.

Christianity today in the United States and the West seems to be losing perhaps not the love for the blessed Theotokos as much as the awareness of her place in the Church. Are there, I wonder, as many special services addressed to her, such as the Akathist prayers, as there were in our past? I believe not. America was founded by sects of northern European Protestants who had no role in worship for the Virgin Mary that was comparable to that of the earlier Church. In our ecumenical outreach it is easier to emphasize Jesus Christ and to ignore the place of the holy Mother of God in Orthodox theology as we attempt rapprochement with other Christians; yet, by doing so we are not being true to the early Church's heritage. A simplistic, fundamentalist version of Christianity scored a coup in our nation by capturing the media through television, radio, and most public religious book stores, scorning and rejecting any thologies not in conformity with its own mode of thought. That, too, is praiseworthy, in that everything that upholds a belief in Jesus Christ is commendable; however, the tradition of identifying with the experiences of Christ's mother in this world and in the next, ought not to be withheld from Christians who empathize with her feelings.

8
Epiphanies of Love

Eat, O friends, and drink; drink deeply, O lovers!
(Song of Songs 5:1)

More than merely eating, a meal is an act of sharing with another, going outside one's self and reaching with one's being to the other.

> "Here, take it..." And he takes altar bread from his kerchief. I recognize it—inexpensive altar bread, out of my childhood—bread of poor folk. Joyfully I take it . . . My God! . . . I remembered. It's the old psalm reader . . . Nicolai Arsentyich, from back home. He came to get me.
>
> *Shadows of Days,* by Ivan Shmelyov

This is an excerpt from the émigré experience of a Russian who had escaped from the Bolsheviks. He took up a life in Paris and felt himself estranged from society. This dream, or vision, came to him to nourish his soul with a fond memory from his childhood. It is a simple man who appears and reaches out to share a portion of the *prosfora* distributed after the Divine Liturgy. What does it cost? Nothing at all, in terms of money, and yet the action of love it expresses is a priceless gift. How many times have each of us venerated the cross and taken a morsel of the blessed bread from the server's tray? How many times have we thought to keep it and share it with another?

Now I think of the nurse who always takes the time to carry a portion of altar bread to those she knows from the hospital register who are Orthodox. What is it but a cube of bread the size of a crouton, dried out by the time it is eaten; and yet the action of love and caring, that gift of sharing, communicates something of what the gospel is about. It announces wordlessly: "You are Christ's, as am I. We are together children of the Savior's Father, His parent by birthright and now our Father by adoption, and in the Holy Name of the heavenly family I came to share with you a reminder of God's love."

We know so little if anything at all about what will take place before the "dread judgment seat of Christ," when we shall all be called to account for the way we conducted ourselves on earth. But could it be that we shall be shown a replay of our lives, some scenes of missed opportunities? Perhaps if we need help, an angel might point out each instance of when we had had a chance to extend love to another creature—not only to humans but to animals, and even to plants—when we failed. Charles Dickens had this in mind when he had crusty old Ebenezer Scrooge transported by his partner Marley's spirit into the past, in the *Christmas Carol.* But we are not so fortunate as to have so clear an illumination of our missed chances to show love; why is it that we are so reluctant to put love into the lives of others? If we were to list the reasons we do not care to share our lives and our things, they might include the following:

My parents taught me to watch out for myself first.
Nobody helps me when I am in need.
I tried to be kind once, but it was not accepted.
Ours is not that kind of society. People are too sophisticated to care for each other nowadays; be-

sides, there are organizations set up for that sort of thing.

I have my own problems. I'm too depressed to probe into somebody else's misery.

Love is for weaklings. I'd rather be tough.

In the real world it's everyone for himself.

I'm too shy to risk the chance that my attempt would be rejected.

Not one of these excuses holds up against the reply that comes from Christ's cross. Try. Take your own excuse for living only for yourself and stand before the cross. Say it to the Savior and listen to the sound of your plea. Do you think it possible to love Jesus, yet not be like Him? If the cross is the supreme evidence of self-emptying, of pouring out one's very blood for the benefit of others, is there some excuse for living a life enclosed in self-interest? And what is being asked of any of us, but to search for ever newer means to bring love to others, to find other living beings who need affection, to make our lives examples of the deeper truth of that telephone commercial, "Reach out and touch someone." To touch them with a kind word, a flower, a card, a note, even a bit of blessed bread—any means that shows you notice they exist and shows that they share God's world with you.

9
Suffering: The Price of Love

If you find my loved one, tell him
I am sick with love.
(Song of Songs 5:8)

Who is there who has not grappled with the problem of suffering, hoping for a way to avoid it? Not mere physical suffering, for we are able to come to a mature understanding that we can bear nearly any pain inflicted upon our bodies, but the suffering that comes with the death of a loved one, which is much more intense.

The ancient Stoic philosophers had a solution based on withholding love, realizing that one day it would hurt if they did not. They recommended not loving. Epictetus in the *Enchiridion* (III) wrote a basic rule: "Kiss your wife and child, show them every mark of affection. But do not love them! If you do, you will be upset if they die."

The renowned philosopher-king Marcus Aurelius, in his ninth meditation, wrote: "Some pray, 'O God, do not take from me my son!' The wise man will pray, 'Let me not be disturbed when he is taken.' "

If the primary value is the self, and the worst happening imaginable is that one suffers, then the Stoic way is the only sure way of mitigating suffering. Christianity never promises that a person will not suffer; on the contrary, we are called up to take our share of suffering like good soldiers (2 Tm

2:3). In fact, there is just no escape from anguish, because suffering is the price one pays for loving.

Our culture today places a supreme value on freedom. Many feel that they must never be restricted from doing whatever they wish. Such unlimited freedom is possible, perhaps, provided a person is able to resist the natural, humanizing need to love.

Our young people today, and in fact all in this society, are offered the hedonistic philosophy of fun and lust, which passes for love, and are told that it can be had at a low price. They pay whatever it costs to make themselves virile and appealing. We have with us the myth personified by James Bond, in which women are merely interchangeable sexual objects varying marginally in looks or hair styling. Women's liberation groups are correct in protesting such male chauvinism, but they offer no truly Christian alternative, something more than the mirror image of the male domination of women. What is set forth as an answer to male chauvinism is the opportunity for women to have the same loveless love they presume men to enjoy.

The result of any victories of women's liberation, therefore, will not be that only the male half of the population, but all "adults," have the "right" to free love—another name for self-gratification without acceptance of the responsibility for the well-being of the other, which true love entails, including the capacity for enduring the trauma of the end of real love, as when death comes, or in the ability to share with the partner all the sorrows that he or she endures in a lifetime.

For the Christian, suffering is a profound mystery, a reality of this world which Christ the God-man endured. Evidently, it is a part of the entire process of redemption, and as such is not intended to lead us to confusion and rebellion, but to our ultimate joy of living with God Himself, and with all who take upon themselves the suffering that accompanies love, living through its trials to conquer at the end.

10
The Reflection of Love

Which way did your loved one go, that
we may look for him with you?
(Song of Songs 6:1)

How I enjoy the many hours I spend in airport terminals. The delight of being there stems from the emotions brought forth from the people who are either parting from one another or greeting arrivals. Those families that take one another for granted are in these circumstances, at least, forced to display their affections, for in a sense each parting is a prelude to death, just as each greeting prepares us for the magnificent reunion that will be realized in the Lord's Kingdom. At airports we rehearse our farewells and our greetings.

After the goodbye hugs and kisses it is those who remain that have the greater melancholy. The airline passengers may turn around and wave adieu, but they have the excitement of the flight and the destination ahead to remove the sadness of parting. Would it not be better to speak of the dead, not in the conventional phrase as the "departed," but rather as the "departing," the way ticket holders are in the terminals?

Immensely happier are those who await the arrival of an incoming flight. I take pleasure in attempting to predict the sort of greeter each one will be by his mannerisms. The ones who bolt forward and bowl over the "arrivee" with a bear hug, or sometimes an airlift, followed by hearty back slaps; the planter, who stands feet apart and arms flayed outward, signifying that the other is obliged to come ahead and receive the gift of a squeeze; the simpering smiler who is uncomfortable with public displays of affection, extending a nervously tight hand; the recluse who backs up against the wall and waves on tiptoes. Once in the Tampa airport I saw three agile young men standing on one another's shoulders in an immense sack draped from the top fellow to the ankles of the support man.

Most vividly, however, I remember returning from Tulsa to my home early one February, passing through a massive snowstorm. Our plane was at least three hours late. The terminal was darkened as we taxied slowly to the gate. From the tiny, ovoid window I could discern only vaguely within the terminal the families of those on board pressing their noses and flattened palms against the windows, gesticulating in their excitement, pointing eagerly to our lumbering vessel. It was before the days when they attached the giant vacuum cleaner exits to the doors of the planes. Passengers disembarked and walked outdoors to the terminal, and in that brief period one could sense the electricity of attachment between those inside the terminal and the ones trudging through the snow.

That, to me, is what heaven will be like. I feel certain that those who "have gone before us to their rest," as we chant liturgically, will be eagerly awaiting that glorious reunion after this life is ended, when our "plane" arrives and we are ushered along through the entry gates of God's glorious Kingdom. But heaven will be more than just a meeting between family and old friends. He who made our access possible, the Savior Jesus Christ, who provided us with passports to His Father's realm, will reveal not only Himself, but the selves we had been intended to become. And our images will be radiant. As Saint John Climacus wrote,

> If the face of a loved one clearly and completely changes us and makes us cheerful, gay and carefree, what will the face of the Lord not do when He makes His Presence felt invisibly in a pure soul?
>
> (*Ladder of Divine Ascent,* 30:16)

11
The Chambers of the Heart

Set me as a seal upon your heart.
(Song of Songs 8:6)

Saint Paul personalized that scriptural plea when he wrote: "It is only right for me to feel this way about you, because I have you all in my heart" (Ph 1:7).

All who have taken even an elementary course in biology were taught that the human heart, like those of many "higher animals," contains four chambers. From the spiritual perspective, however, countless chambers fill that vital organ.

How tragic to consider that there exist human hearts with only a single spiritual chamber. Room for self alone. Persons live and die without sharing their hearts with others. How does it happen? Maybe it might be argued that nobody ever really goes through this world so utterly selfishly that he never thinks of someone else—a parent, at least. But St Paul is referring to the heart's chambers, and not the mind's. We may think of others now and then, we may even thank those who cared for us at various stages in our journey through this world; nevertheless, the mind is teeming with thoughts and memories, with ideas and images constantly rushing in and out, while we are both awake and asleep. But thinking of others is not the same as holding them in our hearts.

At present, science is exploring the frontiers of the

psyche. Scientists have monitored successfully the empathy between identical twins, noting that when a strong emotion seizes one of them, the other experiences a similar feeling. Those who are most in touch with their emotions and who are, at the same time, persons who have a deep and real love for others, sense intuitively when their friends are undergoing traumatic events in their lives. Anyone who has had experiences shared with another person will testify to the truth of these words.

The first chamber of the heart should be occupied by the one we mean when we pray to the Lord, the one who occupies the hearts of those baptized in the Name of Father, Son, and Holy Spirit. They are those who realize the significance of St Paul's words from their own experience: "I live, yet not I, but Christ lives in me" (Ga 2:20).

It is impossible to be at the same time both an ego-maniac and a true Christian, because faith in Jesus is awareness that He is alive, and that His desire is to live in the hearts of all who invite Him to abide with them personally and completely. To live selfishly is to live with a spiritual heart problem, since God made our hearts not only capable of sharing the godliness that Jesus Christ brings us, but also to function authentically only when they are expanding to include Christ. Just as physicians encourage exercise to strengthen the heart's muscular composition, so we Christians must encourage selfless, outgoing acts of love in order to expand the chambers of the heart, so that those chambers will not atrophy but be ever expanding, making room for ever more persons who will be always present within us. The heart in that way will become ever more spiritually healthy and will achieve what it was intended to by its Maker.

12
Love and Death

Love is as strong as death.
(Song of Songs 8:6)

It seems that instinctively we know, not only as human beings, but as organisms like all living creatures, that our ultimate enemy is death. The thought of it remains with us throughout our lifetime, and we deal with it for the most part by suppressing the remembrance of it, or else by convincing ourselves that death is something that happens to other persons, to somebody else's family, but not to us or to ours.

Some take the philosophical approach of fatalism, which says that the length of our lives is determined at our birth, and that since we cannot change or add to it, we must accept it and prepare to meet death whenever it comes. One ancient school taught that we should not indulge ourselves with "fantasies" of a life beyond this one, but by accepting and embracing the limitations of our existence we should greet death heroically, without placating ourselves with "delusions" of an afterlife.

There are those who will not allow themselves to love anyone, because it pains so greatly when the one we love is taken by death. Better, they feel, to keep love at a distance than to bear suffering and grief.

But death has met its match in love, as the beautiful love story in the Song of Songs reveals: Jesus has incarnated that love expressed in a poem, demonstrating the way love's victory has come about. Whenever we make the sign of the cross on our bodies we pass twice over our hearts, showing the heart to be the center of the cross-symbol of God's love for humanity as revealed by Christ's crucifixion.

We glory in the awareness that God loves us more than we are capable of comprehending, but at the same time we remember that we must respond with our own courage, being ever prepared to accept suffering, since love, even God's love, comes with a price.

A Spanish mystic once said, "If you die before you die, you will not die when you die." This has a double meaning: Those who give up on life somewhere on the way to death live dreary, miserable lives filled with emptiness and self-loathing because deep within themselves they cannot suppress the realization that they were given the gift of life as an investment, a treasure not to be wasted or frittered away, but to be made into something worthwhile... and nothing is more worthy of a life well spent than evidence of the love of God expressed toward others. Those who cannot live in love will not be ready for death when it comes, because they have been living a lifeless existence, waiting for something to fulfill their lives, still waiting when death claims them. And death is not an event, but an intruder.

Conversely, if you live in love until the moment you die, you will not die even when you die. Is that not the substance of the Biblical record of life? What victory did Herodias achieve when her daughter Salome brought her John the Baptist's head on a platter, when the spirit of the Baptist so pursued Herod that he thought Jesus was John reincarnated (Mt 14:1-2)? Love for the Lord's justice made St John the Baptist greater than death.

Death is the measure by which we may realize the dimensions of love in a person. "Greater love has no man, than this, that he lay down his life for his friends" (Jn 15:13). The same gospel makes it clear that freedom is at work in the act of true love. Jesus was not compelled to sacrifice His life for the world, just as the blessed Trinity did not have to will that the only begotten Son of God be born a man, suffer, and die for mankind's salvation. Love is like that in its essence: there is no compulsion that traps a person in a relationship. The same "Little Lord Jesus" in the Christmas carol, who "lay down His sweet head," so loved the world that He lay down not merely His head, but His very life in order that we may have a life with Him through love, on the far side of death. Let everybody understand that death is no match for His love.

II. FROM ST PAUL'S HYMN OF LOVE IN FIRST CORINTHIANS

13
The Most Excellent Way

But eagerly desire the greater gifts. And now I will show you the most excellent way . . .
(1 Corinthians 12:31)

St Paul was writing to the Corinthians about spiritual gifts. Chapters 12 and 14 fit together neatly on the subject, so neatly, in fact, that scholars think the poignant hymn of love, chapter 13, was added as an afterthought. A better explanation is that it goes to the heart of what the apostle wished to convey on the subject of spiritual gifts in the Corinthian Church.

He recognized how much they all wanted the benefits of belonging to Christ. They had experienced the power of the Holy Spirit and they were eager to have manifested those blessings within themselves. St Paul had nothing against that desire; after all, Christ Himself encouraged us to "Ask . . . seek . . . knock" (Mt 7:7). He sensed, however, a misunderstanding of those spiritual gifts, a greediness that ignored and refused to develop the simple gifts they already possessed. More, there appeared an exhibitionism of the type we find displayed in our times, now that television encourages such performances, of dramatic faith healings, "slaying in the Spirit," tongue-babbling, and the like.

The blessed apostle sat back and asked himself what word might be added that could speak to the heart of the subject? Yes, the gifts of the Spirit are wonderful, but something even more profound lies at the roots of the gospel of Jesus Christ. The Corinthians were experiencing something like the euphoria felt by the seventy disciples who had been sent out by Christ. Upon returning they stated that "Even the demons submit to us in [Christ's] name." Admonishing them gently, Jesus replied: "Do not rejoice that demons submit to you, but rejoice that your names are written in heaven" (Lk 10:17,19).

The gate of heaven is opened with the key of love. When Christ was asked, "Which is the greatest of all the commandments?" (Mk 12:28), He replied, "Love the Lord your God with all your heart, mind, and strength, and love your neighbor as yourself." Of all the important verbs He might have used—for instance, *believe, sacrifice, pray, fast, obey*—He chose the word *love,* for only love leads us to heaven.

What an exquisite moment, that instant when the Holy Spirit inspired the genius of the apostle to search within himself for the words to put into perspective those divine gifts presented to Christians since the Pentecost event. Love is the measure, and love must head the list of blessings. Only love matters ultimately; only love endures throughout eternity.

To be like God is to love the way God loves and to love everything that the Holy Trinity loves. Unity with the Divine Being is not so much gathering up all the graces that make a Christian different from what he would be by nature, but rather the nurturing of those elements of love that are already in one's soul. Conforming to the likeness of the Lord is to assume an ever greater responsibility for God's creation. How is this facilitated by speaking in tongues? As desirable as that spiritual gift was to the Corinthians, St Paul shows how that charism benefits only the possessor, but does precious little service to anybody else.

Love, conversely, comes from within the soul, and always implies the other, the object of one's love. Implies? Rather, it requires the other, focusing attention on the other person, to the extent of sacrificing one's self so that the other might live and come to know more fully the love of God.

14
Love Words

I may speak in tongues of men or angels, but if
I am without love, I am a sounding gong or
a clanging cymbal.
(1 Corinthians 13:1)

Is it not ironic today to meditate on this image that begins the New Testament's song of love? St Paul refers to a human who sounds like an instrument when he speaks without love. In our time we have developed many such instruments that can "talk": computers that can articulate words in any language, kitchen appliances that announce when the dishes are ready, even automobiles that speak to the drivers—but can this be called communication in the truest sense?

There is more to human expression than words sounded in an articulate pattern. We human beings know the difference. We spend much of our day filtering from our memory banks words that would be messages worth remembering, if we were to allow them access to our attention. For instance, when the telephone rings, we have no idea who is on the line with us. Even after a pleasant voice greets us by name, we are not always sure whether it is an acquaintance or a stranger; however, if the next sentence is "How are you today?" we realize instinctively that our telephone is being used for a sales promotion. Children raised on television early on discern the program fare from the commercials and the soft-sell routines. Voices come from people who talk to us as if to a machine, because they have no care for the object of their discourse. They speak at another, not as to a person, but to a potential sale. In an office, school, or factory the same results can be identified, once the ear is attuned to non-feeling dialogue (or, perhaps more properly, monologue). Persons who talk simply to be relieved of pent-up emotions are not truly communicating; that word has at its root "commune," the term made sacred by the Church to describe the meeting between the Holy Trinity and the person who receives Christ into his or her heart.

To communicate is to send and to receive messages from one heart to another. In our world of superfluous words, we are separated by a common language, because words are such a cheap commodity. With machines that talk like people and people who insist on talking like machines, we flee from words, leaving sense to come to us out of the silence.

To speak with love requires no language skills. Signs and gestures will do. We are subtle creatures—we must be, in order to survive. Our eyes, for example, send signals of inner feelings even beyond our own control. Everybody recognizes what shifty eyes signify. God gave human beings eyes with so much white surrounding the irises so that we might more readily notice if a person is looking at us directly or averting our gaze. A person's pupils dilate when he is interested in what he sees, which is why professional gamblers often wear tinted glasses. This cannot be disguised or controlled. All of us know these signals, often subliminally, even if we fail to raise intuition to our conscious minds. There exists a language of love and acceptance, understanding, and the desire for cooperation with another, just as surely as there exists a language of anger and discord, rejection, and unconcern. The story of the Tower of Babel might be understood as more than merely the distribution of languages among the builders; with a common will and purpose the laborers might have come up with an understandable sign language. Rather, the Bible relates the story of a communications breakdown, conflict of interest, and perhaps disagreement. With their shouting at one another, each insisting on his own way, refusing to accept a common plan and authority—in a word bickering like any society or family when love is absent—communications ended.

But when love accompanies one's words, all recognize the meaning. Those who speak not with guile or flattery, self-praise or intimidation, but with gentleness and concern for the value of the other—these people are clearly understood. They speak not to the ears of the other, but to the heart; and the heart of a human being cannot be deceived so readily. We all can recognize the deceivers, or at least most of us soon catch on, because something inside, the Spirit of truth, helps us to hear what the ear cannot always grasp, measuring the soul of the speaker behind the words.

15
I Love, Therefore I Am

If I have the gift of prophecy and can fathom all mysteries and all knowledge . . . and have not love, I am nothing.
(1 Corinthians 13:2)

We recall the words of Jesus from the famous Sermon on the Mount: "Many will say to me on that day, 'Lord, Lord, did we not prophesy in your name, and in your name drive out demons and perform many miracles?' Then I will tell them plainly, 'I never knew you. Away from me, you evil-doers' " (Mt 7:22). They never knew the loving presence of Jesus, even though they used His sacred name to perform mighty deeds.

"If I have not love, I am nothing." Conversely we might turn that sentence around and state it in a positive manner: Because I have Christ's love abiding with me, I am something, or better, somebody.

The French philosopher Descartes stated those renowned words: "I think, therefore I am" (*cogito, ergo sum*). We prefer to affirm these: *Amo, ergo sum*, "I love, therefore I exist." Descartes is out of fashion among contemporary philosophers, since by identifying existence with the thought processes he separated existing from the elemental functions of the body. People today want to be in touch with their bodies and emotions as well as with their minds. For instance, notice how important physical fitness is to our culture. Thinkers eke out an existence from stipends, grants, and contributions to get through college, but athletes are revered as demigods, commanding millions for their talents. Psychologists and analysts deal not with the mind alone, but rather set out to explore inner emotions, conflicts, and hostilities by releasing them in a controlled environment, so that the inner tensions of the whole person can be dealt with.

Love also embraces the entire being. We do not fall in love intellectually, we do not set our minds on liking one person or another, but we receive a total image of the person and our entire self responds according to the complete impression that the other human being has made upon us: Body (appearance), mind (what they may have said or failed to say), and soul (how we felt in their presence). Love is based on all of these ingredients.

If a human is nothing unless he is filled with love, why is there such a reluctance to love? Can it be due to a lack of trust? Charlatans abound who use the love of another person for ulterior purposes. The media reported the conviction of a man who had married more than seventy-five women just to swindle them out of their savings. Commercial salespersons affect an intimacy in order to make a sale. Persons who are more instinctive at holding people at bay by affecting aloofness do so by not making eye contact, lest they encourage those who would harm them.

St Paul tells us that a prophet can be without love. How can this be? One who can anticipate the future by carefully analyzing the work of God in history ought to be filled with love and compassion, but seeing is not feeling. Elisha was a prophet of God, yet he was so testy that he could not bear to have children tease him (2 Kg 2:23). Satan knew the mysteries of the Holy Trinity, yet his knowledge provoked him to envy. There are many with advanced degrees in our society who have spent a lifetime of study, experts in their disciplines, yet who are without a portion of the love seen in the attendants at nursing homes or institutions for the disadvantaged. Who, indeed, is able to measure love?

16

Where is Love?

If I should prophesy and know all mysteries . . . and have not love, it profits me nothing.
(1 Corinthians 13:2)

The holy Saint Maximus in the seventh century compiled from the writings of the Church Fathers four hundred "chapters," actually paragraphs, on the subject of divine-human love—called in Greek *agape,* and in Latin, *caritas,* from which we derive the term charity. Here is the concluding chapter which he intended as a summary and highlight to all that came before it:

> Many have said much about charity. Looking for it only among the disciples of Christ will you find it, for they alone hold the true Charity, the Teacher of charity, of which it is said, "If I should prophesy and know all mysteries and all knowledge . . . and have not love, it profits me nothing!" [1 Cor 13:2]. He then who possesses charity possesses God Himself, for "God is Love." To Him be glory unto ages of ages. Amen.
>
> (St Maximus the Confessor, *Four Centuries on Charity,* IV:100)

Where else, indeed, should one expect to find true love

but among Christians, since they alone have as Lord and Teacher the very epitome of godly love?

Is he correct? In our world today, can we affirm that blessed, selfless love is manifested by the disciples of Christ? An interesting thought. Does it appear among committed Christians more decisively than among others who go by the name Christian? Do church-goers feel an obligation to love not only one another, but everything on earth that the Father holds dear? Put another way: Might one expect that visitors to our churches would be made aware of love radiating out to them, embracing them within the community of the faithful? Or is that a rather naive presumption?

Yet somehow love always is the measure of belief. One summer I was invited to share a week of faith exchange at an ecumenical setting in Wisconsin. Another guest was a renowned writer on religious themes, a specialist in the cults who took up the cause of the Unification Church led by the Rev. Moon. It impressed me that he would champion them, and I presumed he did so because he was rewarded lavishly for his espousal of its cause, but he insisted he had been drawn to them because of their concern for him as a person. Precisely the attribute that true Christians affirm to be theirs.

"Love is made complete among us," insists the Johannine writer (1 Jn 4:17). "Only among the disciples of Christ will you find it," says St Maximus. Is this literally true, or mere wish-fulfillment? Are these definitions of believers today, or indictments? Do we love, or do we explain why we don't?

After the sixties and seventies, what hasn't been tried in the way of religions? Cults, fads, pseudo-sciences, even nutrition and exercises are made to substitute for religion. But true Christianity has yet to be revealed on a wide scale. If it should come to our civilization as an alternative to hedonism and emptiness, as well it might, the extent of our love will be the test of our worth.

The Greeks were converted to Christ by the irrefutable logic of the Christian doctrine. The Russians were captivated by the splendor of sacred worship. But the average American is not generally won over by a commanding, overwhelming dogmatic theology, and does not seem to be overly impressed by lavish liturgics.

Honesty, consistency, an integrity of life that takes into account all that a person is, does, and believes—this is the mark of faith commonly accepted by most Americans today. They will not tolerate hypocrisy, mendacity, or vacillation, even if they would not say it that way. "Sincerity" is the basic value moderns are searching for in a religious leader and in a church. They will take no less than an open, loving, caring, sharing spiritual community. This is the haven for which the nation yearns.

Does American Christianity meet those specifications, and if not now, might it do so in the near future? Hear the plea captured in a song from the musical "Oliver"; for not only Americans but the entire world is asking, "Where, O where is love?" If it is to be found among us we shall grow and multiply, but if not, the world will continue searching. It's as simple and as difficult as that.

17
Sweet Mystery of Love

If I . . . can fathom all mysteries . . . but have not love, I am nothing.
(1 Corinthians 13:2)

The long search of his mind extended far beyond the imaginative capacity of most humans in any generation. St Paul truly was a prodigy of theology. Most modern theologians begin and end with the evidence of revelation, never daring to presume to speculate over transcendent matters, yet Paul implies that even though it is possible to know the mysteries God has now made known to the world, such as the relations to one another in the future Kingdom of Heaven (Mt 13:11) or the details of humanity's redemption (Rm 16:25), that knowledge will be of no avail to us if we lack love.

But Orthodox Christians use the word *mystery* in another way. We prefer it to that with the Latin root, *sacrament.* In that sense, our liturgy and order of service can be called mysteries, and we might then apply this warning directly to ourselves.

Christian rituals are extremely significant. Clergy are often measured by their knowledge of the intricate, elaborate services most hold in reverence. Many priests have a fixation on the structure and style of worship, at times nearly to obsession. More significant than preaching the gospel is the enactment of the worship, at least for some. And yet, all of it can be of little value when it is performed mechanically, coldly, without the feeling of love.

Nothing is more difficult to excuse or to explain to visitors than evidence of ritual performances without warmth or conviction. Rubricists who know the formulae of the various books of prayer, what every symbol signifies, technicians in the ever more rarefied specialty of liturgical composition, preserve the form of our public prayers, yet only feelings nourished with the constant supply of loving response to God's love can infuse the mysteries with content.

I should like to be assured that all who pray publicly in churches realize the significance of love in the performance of eucharistic and other worship services of the Church. When concerned persons discuss the needs of the present in terms of language alone or structure, or content, I feel those modifications are missing the point. An injustice is being done to our communicants who are certainly capable of discerning when they are witnessing a love affair between the Lord and those who are growing in their knowledge and love for the Holy Trinity, and when they are being invited to participate in an empty ceremony performed but not experienced in the hearts of those who read the words of prayer.

Faith itself witnesses to a profound mystery of love. Somehow, for reasons that transcend mere human logic, the God who made us also loves us in spite of all we have done to thwart, ignore, and abuse that love. He loves us, even though we cannot even adequately begin to reciprocate that affection. He loves us despite ourselves. We do not earn that love by performing the right rites, nor can we take for granted our place in God's Kingdom because of our baptism, or any of the subsequent spiritual mysteries we have been part of. God loves us freely, but we must not presume upon that love; rather, it is for us who are loved to love in return the Almighty Lover, and all that He loves as well.

18
To Give With Love

If I give all I possess to the poor . . .but have not love, I gain nothing.
(1 Corinthians 13:3)

A powerful admonition, and difficult to fathom. Imagine selling all of one's possessions, giving the proceeds to the poor, yet receiving no blessing from it, no ultimate benefit, only because it had not been done for love. Is this merely hypothetical? Is St Paul imagining such a scenario just to make a strong case for his understanding of love?

Remember the gospel story of the rich ruler (Lk 18:18) who thought he wanted to inherit eternal life until Jesus informed him it would cost him at least all of his wealth. He was unable to give to the poor; therefore, Jesus said nothing about love, although we might infer that one lesson at a time should be sufficient. Love would come in due course, for in self-surrender and commitment to Christ, the love that radiated from the Lord would infiltrate the souls of His true followers and bring them to the point of loving all those who are adored by the Lord. Not all of His followers, however, were so inspired by the example of Jesus, as we realize in the case of Judas Iscariot.

Charity (*caritas*) is the Latin term for that type of self-giving love; we use that word to describe any contribution to the needy. But charity as we know it is not necessarily qualified by love. Put simply, "United Appeal" surely would not insist that our love accompany our donations. Let it be a tax write-off; what's wrong with that? We separate the inner feelings of the giver from the contributions he makes, since we recognize it is possible to give a donation without giving ourselves in the process. The brilliant Jewish philosopher Moses Maimonides listed eight ways of giving, in ascending order according to their worth:

1. To do so reluctantly, regretting the donation even as we make it;

2. To give happily, but not generously, making a token contribution yet failing to meet the complete amount required;

3. To meet the full request, but only after the person in need is forced to plead and implore his case;

4. To make the gift willingly, without any need for entreaty, but not secretly; rather, placing the contribution in the hand of the needy in the presence of others, shaming him in the process;

5. To give in such a way that the donor will not know the receiver, while the receiver does know who has helped him;

6. To make the offering through a third party, in order that the recipient not know his benefactor;

7. To establish an agency for charity that will solicit anonymous funds and distribute them according to a program, without notifying either the offeror or the benefactor. In the past, Church poor boxes acted in this manner. Today this activity is taken up by Church-affiliated and secular social welfare agencies;

8. The loftiest way of charity is to anticipate and to head off any need for charity, by seeing to it that a

person does not become a pauper or in debt, either by finding him employment or by putting him in touch with the means to meet his own financial obligations.

We must read the Scriptures in light of the above, because elements within Christianity rightly concerned with the welfare of humanity would reduce the gospel to the work of charity. Salvation is at the heart of Christ's message, not merely social improvement. As beautiful a human concern as the welfare of our neighbors can be considered a modern heresy if it usurps the gospel message, reducing the plan of the Holy Trinity for all the children of Adam and Eve to improving the conditions for happiness on earth. The love of God that makes us godlike, reaching to us and to other persons must accompany our every good deed if it is to be lasting.

19
The Spirit of Patient Endurance

Love is patient . . .
(1 Corinthians 13:4)

St Paul puts love above every other virtue. More important than knowledge, wisdom, prophetic insight, or compassion, lasting longer than faith and hope, love is the gift we cannot ever be without, either in this world or in the Kingdom of God that awaits us. After stating how significant love is, he proceeds to describe it for us. The first attribute the eloquent apostle mentions is patience. All expressions of love ought to be characterized by that quality, yet this is more than most humans are capable of, unless they possess the grace of God.

Patience, as the Christian practices it, has nothing to do with resignation, the acceptance of what we disapprove of, while knowing we cannot change. That is fatalism, and Christians are in principle realistic optimists—realists, for we know quite well the sinful, fallen state of the world which others may call "natural," yet optimists, for we proclaim our conviction that despite all that appears to our earthly eyes to the contrary, God is working out a plan for the salvation of those who desire to be united with the Holy Trinity. In other terms, patience is a positive trait, confirming the effect that time has on a person's behavior. To be patient is to understand that God takes a lifetime to mold a human being into His own image. We must always bear in mind the entire process, even though we cannot fathom what it is that God is refining and fashioning, which may come to fruition in the sunset years of life.

The prototype of patience, or that wonderfully descriptive synonym "long-suffering," we find in the way God deals with the people He chose to bear witness to Him in the Old Testament. They seem forever to be falling into sin and trying the Lord's patience, yet He is endlessly willing to take them back and give them another chance at virtuous behavior.

That godlike quality we cannot be without, and we must exercise every opportunity to put it into effect in our relations with one another. No parent can be good without patience. Child-rearing is a sequence of trials, and the impatient parent is guaranteed to fail. Infancy, toddler days, pre-school, puberty—all have their challenges and strains, demanding an abundance of patience, yet the period of the teens is probably the time more than all others when a parent's love and endurance are put to the test. A charming bumper sticker reflects that truth: "Hire a Teenager Today—While He Still Knows Everything!"

If a parent is to fail it is probably at that period, when he/she insists that the young adult return to the docile, unquestioning stage of earlier years. The parent wants to know "Where did I go wrong," but the question goes unanswered, since it fails to take into account the process of maturation. Nicodemus was right in doubting that a life can return to the womb (Jn 3:4). Adolescence is a transitory stage of life, calling for toleration from the youth as well as the parent. God is molding not a child, not an adult (in the "for adults only" sense), but a being He wants to unite with Himself. Life is that process, and we must ever bear in mind that we are limited in knowing what we are intended to be; therefore, it is for us to be facilitators one to another, aiding in the process, rather than demanding that another do what is our will. If we are able to pray, "Be patient, God is not yet through with me," then surely we can demonstrate long-suffering and tolerance with each other.

20
The Gift of Patience with Patients

Love is patient.
(1 Corinthians 13:4)

I spend a great deal of time in various nursing homes. They are a fact of life nowadays, and families who formerly would have ruled out without discussion the institutionalizing of a parent realize that situations develop which make it exceedingly difficult to give proper care to a loved one. How do they choose from the many nursing homes they visit? Appearance, probably, is a factor. Location as well, to be near for visits; and, certainly, price. Once inside, they should listen sceptically to the interview with the staff officer as well as the persons on the tour. To me, nursing homes are as varied as ordinary homes. Each has a flavor of its own. One can determine the aura of the place from the way the people, staff, and patients communicate with each other.

It has to do with love, and that's an individual quality. The administration sets the tone. Most are officious, probably trying to imitate a conventional hospital if possible. Sometimes they seem cloyingly obsequious or patronizing, as if old people are always senile. Others, the worst kind, maintain a quasi-funereal atmosphere, where all seem to whisper to one another and the patients are either convinced or induced to exist as passively as possible. But love can break through any administrative set of rules and discipline.

I don't know if the rules for admission admit or encourage interviewing in privacy the floor attendants, but that is precisely what I should insist upon before my relatives were admitted to any institution. The people directly in touch with the patients will make the experience either tolerable or miserable.

Of course it requires patience to deal with elderly who experience the natural functional losses that come with the aging process. Everybody should understand that, including the attendants, yet they will be the ones most in touch with those who will try the patience of everybody around them, not merely for an hour of a visit, but daily, minute by minute.

One must comprehend that the elderly live in a different time frame. For them, the past is glitteringly alive, while the present is to be endured and tolerated. They never cease telling stories that happened in "their" day, which obviously is not the present. How ironic it is that what nowadays we call primitive cultures held their elders in high honor, treasuring them as living historians who honed and refined cult legends in endless retelling. Today, we have precious little time to sit and listen.

They forget easily. This ought not be held against them. They drop things. Their coordination is not as functional as it was in the prime of their lives. Because of it, and the slower pace they must maintain, they are easily embarrassed. I find that role reversal comes about with aging, in the sense that when we are young we are taught to defer to our elders, but deep inside the elderly there is a sensitivity that defers to the young. When youngsters treat the aged with openness, not patronizing them or approaching them as infants, the older person feels self-respect and importance. Dignity is affirmed. One is treated as a person, not as a case or a character.

Finally, most important is the resource of precious time which the elderly have more of than younger persons, and which the Church ought to exploit. We believe in the power of prayer. We plead that we "never have enough time" to pray as we should. Can we not approach our respected elders, imploring them to pray, giving them lists of needs that only the Lord can meet? Should we not implore our dear ones who will be entering the Kingdom before us to pray for us, for this broken, ailing world, for the welfare of our Holy Church, and for the unity of all humanity? If prayer is the sure antidote to sin, let us tap this precious resource that we now allow to languish in nursing homes, to do little more than fantasize over times long gone, patiently biding time before the great journey that lies ahead.

21
Binding Kindness to Love

Love is kind.
(1 Corinthians 13:4)

Kindness—so simple a term that we pass it by without a thought. Obvious. Kindness is like water—we take it for granted until we notice it by its absence. Those with little kindness in their personalities demand it from others. In fact, more so than the naturally kind. In Shakespeare's time "kind" had a deeper meaning. He put in Hamlet's mouth his first words: "A little more than kin, and less than kind." Blessed are the children of loving parents, who assume that everybody will treat them as they are dealt with at home. Alas, how unlikely that will be.

It will not happen because our world is fragmented with alienation and self-affirmation. The two are a pair. As the ego makes demands upon others, it loses the ability to understand the other as one who also has needs, creating a division that results in a barrier. Continuing the pursuit of demanding one's own way will multiply that process of offending others, until the egomaniac finds himself alone.

The term "kind" is related to the old English term for family, *kin.* A kind person is one who sees in everybody else a member of his own family and loves her as a sister. Nobody is an alien to a kind person. The measure of kindness is the ability to transcend every element that would appear to cause a separation from one's self: age, sex, color, race, state of health, personal traits, or ideologies. To be able to do that, one must grow in the type of love St Paul writes about. It is not the demanding self-love that satisfies one's ego and ignores the needs of others, certainly, but a self-giving, sacrificial love, that which is best displayed by Christ's cross. There is the supreme act of kindness, manifesting a love that treats all others, enemy and friend, living, departed and yet to be born as "kin," despite the hatred and violence poured out upon Him.

For us it means that the unkind will find no place in heaven. Yes, Christ showed His love for us while we were self-serving egotists who cared nothing for anybody else, but we cannot remain in that state of hostility and self-gratification and at the same time be accounted members in the family of love. That would be no love at all, even if the same term is used in the English language.

For the aggressors in this society kindness may be sentimental, but for Christians it is strength; after all, is it more mature to insist on one's rights or to come to terms with another through understanding his reasoning? Kindness is not weakness. The weak person surrenders his position and accepts another's will as his own. This eventually results in anger, frustration, self-hatred, and an inner alienation from one's oppressor, which is the other side of self-willed ego-assertion. In fact, the weak person cannot be kind easily, since he is not able to escape the imprisonment he brought upon himself by surrendering to his intimidator, who is certainly not "family" in the true sense (although one family member may crush the spirit of a relative, preventing kindness to pass between them).

Kindness involves empathy. Those who love animals realize in them the cravings for basic needs not dissimilar to those of human beings—affection, praise, attention, rewards for good behavior or achievements—and they comprehend the elements of unity underneath the obvious distinctions between species.

When we announce liturgically, "Let us love one another," we affirm our intent to be kind to one another, treating each other as true kin. We are eternal family members who care, who share, and who feel the pain of the sufferer, the grief of the bereaved, the anguish of the disconsolate, the loneliness of the widow and the wretchedness of the self-alienated, as well as the joy of those in touch with the image of God within and feelings of those who surround them. Kindness is love, and without it one cannot be a lover.

22
The Source of Patience and Kindness

Love is patient and kind.
(1 Corinthians 13:4)

How delicately the writings on love in the Bible compliment one another. The author of 1 John notes: "God is love, and the one who abides in love abides in God, and God abides in him" (4:16). St Paul elaborates on the character of God's love: It is always patient and kind. The two are in accord, as the Father and Son are, for the Father in heaven has immeasurable patience with the world, especially with us human beings—not, surely, out of need, as though He could not do otherwise, but rather because He has the entire outline of the world's historical process set forth before Him.

Patience can only come with the kind of perspective a believer has who realizes that God does indeed "Look down from heaven and behold from the heights where [He] dwells holy and glorious" (Is 63:15). Everything takes place in time according to the Lord's plan. We are mere mortals who live in a continual sequence of present moments, not connecting all the events of the past with the present, much less knowing what the future will bring about, and having little of the holy patience. A contemporary author initiated his autobiography with the desire to capture something of the fleeting moments of life, since he did not believe either in God or in the possibility that he himself would exist in any form after this life came to an end. He began his book with these words:

> The cradle rocks above an abyss, and common sense tells us that our existence is but a brief crack of light between two eternities of darkness.
>
> (Vladimir Nabokov, *Speak, Memory*)

Those who believe in God, on the other hand, learn to trust less in the power of their own memories and more in the mind of the Lord; they recognize that "common sense" can deceive them by limiting their sight to the darkness that surrounds them, and fails to take into account the inner light that illuminates the pathway to the true life beyond the existence we call "life." As we grow spiritually, we shed that mortal way of understanding and open ourselves to God's plan for all creation, especially for the unique place human beings hold in that plan. As that reality grows within us, patience accompanies the insight that the Lord is in control, not only of our lives, but of all that exists. Indeed, what exists is deceptive, for we see it as a photograph of permanency, a "still shot" without connection to what preceded or what shall follow. What really exists, however, is more like a motion picture that is changing constantly, evolving, becoming, receiving its meaning from its place in time.

Just as impatience breeds short tempers, patience brings forth the fruits of kindness. If we grow toward assimilating the patience of the Father, we shall incorporate into ourselves the kindness of the Son. The very term St Paul uses for kindness contains in the Greek the title of Jesus, "Christos." But to develop patience and kindness will require much grace from the Holy Spirit, for the temper of our times is in conflict with those holy virtues. In our day, secular culture actually encourages impatience as a mark of somebody on the rise. One who is not hesitant to step over others to make a way upward in the world, who looks on kindness as weakness, who is prepared to change everything regardless of whom he hurts in the process—such is the characteristic of the persons our society cultivates.

Can people in today's world be patient and kind? Only if they are strong enough to absorb what will come to them in return for demonstrating Christian virtues, if they are able to tolerate not being repaid in kind by an unkind, rude, hostile, short-tempered society. To be Christian today is to be prepared to do battle, using the weapons of peace, love, patience, and kindness, knowing that tensions will form deep within one's soul, since those holy virtues challenge the "common sense" of a society that lives by standards other than those of Jesus Christ. St John Chrysostom once stated that if a person is patient only because he or she feels helpless to do otherwise and not out of an inner strength that comes from knowing the Lord's love, then patience will only lead to bitterness. Perhaps it should not be called patience at all, but rather frustration at a world gone awry. Patience comes from knowing one is loved by God, chosen to live forever with the Holy Trinity in the company of saints and angels, called on earth to set an example for those with lesser values for what is possible for a person filled with the grace of the Holy Spirit.

23
True Love is Self-Acceptance

Love is not jealous or boastful.
(1 Corinthians 13:4)

The love the apostle writes about is godly love from the Father, a gift to us by Jesus Christ and therefore unlike the love we experience here on earth, unless that love is similarly infused with the Holy Spirit abiding in both partners. When a relationship is not filled with grace, however, earthly love steps into its place and with it comes either jealousy or boasting.

Jealousy is distressing because the victim feels deprived of love. A jealous person is always measuring himself against others. In the family, it is with his sisters and brothers, against whom he vies for the attention of the parents. In the community, it is where he sets himself against those in similar situations and occupations: students in class, workers in the same office, or professionals in a common career. A person filled with envy will never be able to love himself in the proper way. He will find it difficult to thank the Lord for the life he was given, because he is disappointed with who he is. He considers himself a failure. Somebody is always ahead of him, and he will never find true happiness because of it.

Boasting is the other side of jealousy, revealing a similar limitation of outlook. The braggart measures himself against one he considers inferior to himself. He gloats at his imagined superiority, blind to the likelihood of the many who excel in the area of his supposed dominance, but he does not measure himself against the more advanced. Such a person has a low horizon, seeing only the presumed inferiors, without whom the boaster has no foil.

True love does not measure itself against others in this pitiful human fashion which gives birth to either jealous self-haters or haughty, arrogant boors, because there is no way to measure the love of God. With what instrument are we able to span the effect Jesus' cross had on the world? Despite all the modern devices to gauge distances between celestial bodies or the number of atoms in a molecular field, we have nothing that would calculate the evidence or the intensity of divine love.

The tragedy of envy and boasting lies in the fact that neither type of person afflicted with those weaknesses ever comes to learn from the lessons and experiences of life on this earth; that is to say, the kind of person God had in mind when man was uniquely created. To go through this world measuring one's self by what we see of others is to miss finding out who "I" am. How will I possibly discover that person if I do nothing more than compare myself against others, either despairing that I do not match up to somebody else, or else convinced that I need no further improvement, since I know who my inferiors are and place myself above them.

Contrast the human dimension in a musical performance written for a soloist. Regardless of the number of artists who play the same opus on similar instruments, the solo will be original, differing from every other rendition. Each professional renders an idiomatic performance, rarely attempting to duplicate another's interpretation. In similar fashion, each of us must respect our individuality which was custom made by the divine Lord, and not live as an imitation of somebody else's personality.

More than just a good idea, this truth about the search

for the unique individuality of each human being is solid Orthodox theology, reflecting what true Christians believe to be the sacred duty of each person. Self-discovery is the ongoing search for the image of God in which we have been created.

24
The Gift of Love

Love is not jealous or boastful . . .
(1 Corinthians 13:4)

Jealousy and boasting are character traits of opposite personality types, yet they have a common element. Both have to do with possession. The jealous person is either afraid of losing a lover's affection, or envious of others who are in love with one another, sharing a love that leaves the jealous one out. A person who boasts of a conquest of love is assuming he possesses the heart of another. He owns her, so to speak, in the sense of dominating her thoughts and affections.

True love, on the other hand, can be neither boastful nor jealous for the same reason—such love is a gift from God. One is possessed by the Lord's love, sharing in it, but not exclusively. That would be cause for envy, if we were to take offense at the mystical pouring forth of God's love upon all whom He created, as though it in some manner diluted the love He has for the individual. The older brother of the Prodigal Son fits that description (Lk 15:39).

To boast that one is loved by God is equally absurd, since nothing we have done could merit that love. Spiritual love originates in the Holy Trinity. In fact, the enigma is why the Lord would desire to love such poor, inadequate sinners. What is there in any of us that makes us lovable? But He does love every one of us individually, and that should overwhelm us with gratitude and awe.

Sigmund Freud has been attacked by Erich Fromm and others for misleading western civilization in the proper understanding of love; justly so, for his influence has thwarted the depths of loving, distorting our conception of interpersonal relationships. Freud thought of love as a limited quantity. He stated that after birth we love our mothers to such an extent that we go on searching for mother substitutes in later life, that is, if the initial relationship had been satisfying. Otherwise, we search out her opposite if we reject her love and influence. In either case, love is something we transpose from one object to another.

Christians who experience the overwhelming, constant, and consistent love of the Holy Trinity realize the priority of the heavenly Father's love for His only begotten Son. In fact, we glory in the love that the Father and Son share, because by the Holy Spirit we are made aware of its effect upon ourselves. All this is revealed so tenderly in chapters 15 and 16 of the Johannine Gospel. We bask in the glow of the love the divine Father and Son have for one another in the way we enjoy the heat and warmth of the sun's energy, without having earned it. Yes, God loves each of us, but it can only be a mutual love to the extent that we are capable of conquering sin in ourselves and opening our beings to ever greater degrees of His love for us. This is a sacred love, of which St Paul writes to his students in the faith.

Even on the human level it is illogical for us to be jealous of God's love for other beings: non-Christians, Christians, Orthodox, the saints, and much less for Jesus Himself, although diabolically such envy is certainly possible. But if we love God and it pleases Him to love all that He created and if He is even happier when His love is acknowledged and reciprocated, should we not be pleased whenever God is delighted? And if, because of our sinful nature we have been little more than part-time lovers of the Lord, ought we therefore to be offended when we recognize that others have sacrificed more of themselves for the desire of realizing the love of God, who appreciate His love more than we and who give themselves night and day to serving and praising His glory? Dare we permit the demon of envy to snatch away even the tiny particle of love we have come to share with the blessed Trinity? Not at all, for God's love is not quantitative. He has an inexhaustible supply that He urges each of us to assimilate as much as we are able; therefore, it is ludicrous to envy the portions others delight in, just as it would be silly to boast of what we have not earned or deserved, but which comes to us because it is God's nature to love. As St Irenaeus of Lyons once wrote, "God created man in order to have someone on whom to shower His love."

25
Requirements of Love

Love is not rude, it is not self-seeking, it is not easily angered, it keeps no record of wrongs.
(1 Corinthians 13:5)

To follow Jesus it is not enough to pray to Jesus. One must be like Him as much as possible. This means bearing one's cross, which is immeasurably more than wearing a cross on a chain around the neck. Many are they who are rude, touchy, harboring a list of offenses already years old against those who did them injury in the past, who await the day when all of them will "get what's coming to them" for all the suffering and misery they caused our "Christians," who feel themselves elected to God's Kingdom and have nothing more to do than to go through the unpleasant experience of death in order to reap their reward on the other side.

How simple it would be if we were to heed the call "Follow me," assuming we were doing precisely that in our own private ways. That is the gospel, of course; however, it follows an important requirement. Christ said just prior to the invitation: "Take up *your* cross daily..." (Lk 9:23). Cross-bearing means that we are to bear with rudeness and not reply in kind. St John Chrysostom reminded us that Jesus is the shepherd of sheep and not of wolves; therefore, when we turn ourselves into wolves to fight back against vicious attacks, know that we are without

Christ. Jesus is not battling with us, since we have chosen to forsake His teachings and example to go it alone, in the way of the world.

We move even farther away from Christ when we utilize every opportunity to serve ourselves, for this is not the way of the Lord. In America a popular form of Christianity appeals precisely to the greedy nature of humanity, promising that by giving one's self to Jesus, all the pleasures of this earth will suddenly follow: money, success, power, virility, popularity—once "you turn yourself over to the Lord." Such confusion of the Lord's benefit with this world's concerns is far from the true spirit of godliness.

"Love is not easily angered." Measure your own provocation level when you are driving in heavy traffic. Another simple test is at the checkout counter of the supermarket. When you lose your temper, you also lose touch with the indwelling Christ. St Maximus the Confessor, writing in the seventh century, insisted, "Cleanse your mind of anger, grudges, and shameful thoughts. Then you will be able to know the indwelling of Christ" (*Four Centuries on Charity,* IV:76).

The modern, weak Christian would prefer to do his Christian witnessing another way. He first acts like a pagan and a savage, losing his temper, throwing a tantrum, leaving the scene of a provocation with bitter, resentful thoughts, then after the fact, he pleads a blessing from the Lord. But the Lord never promised us He would be an indulgent nanny, patching up our ego wounds.

Each situation that tests our spirituality is a challenge to our faith. Are we truly cross-bearers, or are we frauds? Do we have the abiding presence of Christ in each situation of our daily lives, or is our faith something ceremonial, reserved for Sunday mornings and brief snatches of prayer on the margins of the day?

Christ is limited by His holiness and purity. He simply cannot abide in us alongside anger, lust, deceit, bitterness, and the like, and we deceive ourselves if we pretend that God's goodness will automatically overcome the sinfulness within us. On the contrary, we are free beings who are able to choose to serve evil rather than God. We may feel we are with Christ by virtue of our baptism or because of His love for us, but that is not the case as long as we have not surrendered our wills to the will of the heavenly Father and have not invited Christ into our hearts. Be sure you comprehend the difference.

26
If You Love Me

Love does not insist on its own way.
(1 Corinthians 13:5)

All young people in their teens and twenties must come to terms with a basic question related to sexuality: Will they maintain their purity for their wedding, or will they give it away prematurely? That problem does not change, whatever society may conclude regarding the differences between one generation and another. If, as in the past, the subject is not discussed openly or, as in the present, it is talked to the point of boredom, each young person must still make the decision for her or himself.

There are changes that take place in time. I had begun writing as if to address young women, when it came to mind that with the so-called "new morality" young men are now propositioned as well as girls, and not necessarily by the girls. We've come a long way, maybe. But the proper response is just the same in every generation, and every Christian young person knows it quite well: NO. After all the arguments and attempts to validate sin, and despite the justification our society sets before the weak-willed, virtue is a two-letter word.

Will there be a time when boys will not desire to test their own sex appeal, goaded on by what they think is masculinity? And is there another "line" more useful than "If you really loved me..."

How does a girl counter that plea? If she is a Christian she will affirm her conviction that premarital sex is a sin no matter how it is explained away, and there are no exceptions to the rule. She will tell her friend that as much as she loves him, she loves Jesus first. In fact, she will say that she loves herself more, and if his ardor requires more slaking, she might think to read him the book of love, the Bible, starting with 1 Corinthians 13.

"Love does not insist on its own way." Here is something beneficial that might even be endorsed by the woman's liberation movement, affirming one's own right to be respected and acknowledged as an equal. Even if the couple are to be married, the implication from forced sex is that in the dance of life he will always lead and she will forever do the following. No, marriage is more than male dominance and female submissiveness; it is a partnership of lovers.

Lust insists on its own way, but if that is the basis for a relationship it will last as long as the urge impelling it, and not much longer. Love and lust are commonly confused in this society, since we have been sated with sexuality as though it were the highest value attainable. We have been deceived into believing the lie that "free love" is available and possible, but we end by learning what every generation and people has come to realize: "Free love" is extremely expensive, and it is nearly always the woman who pays the bill.

"If *you* love *me*," her reply ought to counter, "then you will find joy in maintaining my purity. You will want to see the light of innocence in my eyes through my wedding veil, and you will notice how I shall hold my head up high, worthy to wear white on my wedding day. I have a most precious gift which I intend to give to my husband, and he may well be you; but whoever he is, I wish to honor him with my whole self, and nobody else. Old fashioned? I think not, for I was fashioned by God's love, and His love never goes out of style. He loves me and trusts me; in fact, He put His own image into me, and I intend to polish it until it will shine and glisten like a brilliant wedding crown. I do hope you understand—but if not, then at least understand that I believe all I have said . . . and I intend to live by my convictions."

27
The Candle Snuffer

Love bears all things.
(1 Corinthians 13:7)

Is it not asking more than we are prepared to offer, even in the name of love, to "bear all things"? Is it reasonable, if we are to speak sensibly and not in some fantasy language, to allow another person to abuse us, even mentally, when he refuses to talk to us? Certainly few psychologists would advise that we "bear all things," even from our spouses—not in this day, in any case. What is liberation all about, if not to stand up for our rights? But psychologists concern themselves with adjusting a person to this world. The true Christian who is prepared to give himself to Christ will find that little of the old self and its coping mechanisms will be helpful in the new life with the Lord. For him, liberation has another meaning from the definition this world presumes. It has little to do with political systems or social situations. Rather, it calls for being free of the need to react to any provocations. While we are in this world, we are enslaved by any stimulus: a person, an animal, a nasty letter, even the weather can cause us to respond in some fashion. Christ is showing us how to be free within ourselves, so that even if we are in prison and abused, we need not surrender our basic person to our captors. Is that not the lesson of Christ's last day on earth? Nobody was able to taunt or provoke Him into losing His composure—not His captors, not the Sanhedrin, not Annas, not even the cruel Roman soldiers who thrashed Him mercilessly and put Him to death on the cross.

We are called in the name of love to be like that. Sometimes those who do not know us well and, indeed, even our own people think that these demands made on Orthodox Christians are platonic; not for everybody, but simply a well-meaning vague ideal to hold up as the maximum to which we ought to aspire, but in fact one which nobody, especially inhabitants of today's world, really expects of a person—at least, of those outside monastery walls.

Such a premise would be tragically wrong. One point the Church has insisted on throughout the centuries is that there are not two classes of believers, ordinary folk, and clergy and the monastics. Quite the contrary. Christ came to make us one in every way, and to tear down all false barriers to our unity.

Also, the demands of love, such as to "bear all things," are not a private matter between the individual and God. If we are Christians, then we are on the Lord's side, ready to implement His plan of action for saving the world. Each time we are ignited by the fire of anger that is rampant throughout society, we are presented with a choice: Either we react instinctively and spread the flame, becoming a wick that incorporates that violent passion into our selves, or we can be like the humble candle snuffer, a cap set against the flame which holds the fire, containing it by not allowing it to nourish itself until it slowly extinguishes itself.

This is the way the world will be restored to its Creator. We, who claim to comprehend the meaning of Jesus' title, as Second Adam, ought to realize our roles in turning the world back to Paradise. Impossible? Perhaps, if we fail to take into account the gift of God we call grace. But for the mind of a true Christian, impossibility is a term that does not compute. Not accidentally did St Paul insist on "all." Not little things, not the ordinary things only, not even most things, but everything that is set as an obstacle to attaining the Kingdom of Heaven must be conquered by the grace that is manifested in love. The Christian candle snuffer, not by natural capabilities, but by utilizing all the grace the Lord provides, an inexhaustible, irresistible, and unconquerable divine power, must take every opportunity to smother with love every form of incendiary passion that wages war against the peace and harmony of a restored universe, from the tiny irritations and annoyances wrongly considered ordinary events, to the grotesque, incalculable inferno of nuclear warfare.

28
Protective Love

Love bears all things . . .
(1 Corinthians 13:7)

The distinguishing mark of true love is to protect the other, the object of our love, from harm, shame, or terror. Recall the unpleasant incident of Noah, after having sampled the quality of his new wine to the point of intoxication (Gn 9:20). Ham, first noticing him naked, called his brothers to come and see. They, on the other hand, entered the father's tent backwards and covered their father's shame with a garment. Their love spared Noah embarrassment.

No marriage will last without the same sort of sensitivity manifested by Noah's two sons. Incidents multiply from the wedding day, when one partner notices the failings of the mate. This is normal, for we see the faults of another person much more clearly than we do our own. But what do we make of the awareness? Do we simply ignore it? Do we fault ourselves for having been teamed with somebody with failings? Or do we try to aid the other, covering over the weakness if necessary, in order to protect him or her from embarrassment while we search for the proper time and terms to help in mending the defect of character?

The term for "bear," *stegei,* means "to cover over," as in the Noah episode. This is why newlyweds prefer to live apart from their parents, since under their own roof they are able to find protection for dealing in private with the traits of character they discover in one another.

The Church is intended to be such an extended family under a common roof, where members deal with one another's behavior not by scorn and criticism, but through careful selection of phrases designed to protect the feelings of the other person. Not to disseminate falsehood or to speak untruthfully, recalling the scriptural admonition to "tell all the truth with love," but to hold both parts together at all times. Yes, tell the truth. In fact, decide always to tell the whole truth to one another; leave out nothing, but speak always with love. Never hurt or do injury to the heart and soul of the other.

The other sense of the term, besides protection, is the bearing of all things that do injury. Again in the marriage, each ought to remember that he or she is bound to the other for a lifetime. What the couple is like at the time of marriage is something different from what they will become by their golden wedding anniversary. Each will change, and both will evolve together. That transformation from what is into what will be involves a process, during which time patience is a primary requisite.

If each partner can simply bear with the faults of the other, hope stays alive. The negative features can change, leave altogether, or at least be controlled with maturity, and more positive features will emerge.

Think of any person known to be tender and loving, filled with compassion, and you will discern the quality of bearing with the faults of others. Not because they fail to notice the flaws of character; in fact, they see them more clearly than most, because they have within them the grace to love without the need to judge. The common sinner demands from God justice for others, yet mercy for himself. He has no patience with the failings of all he recognizes in his society who disregard or do not live up to the laws of the Bible and the Constitution. He insists they ought to be put in prison. But when he is found guilty of misbehaving, it comes with an explanation. Then, one must understand the circumstances. So it is with the world, but not with the people of the Lord. Those who belong to Christ are firm with themselves but merciful to others. If the Lord Almighty is able to endure the sins of humanity, surely His servants should be able to do likewise.

29
Standing or Falling in Love

Love never ends . . .
(1 Corinthians 13:8)

When it is said that Christianity fails to communicate with the modern generation, what is meant is not necessarily that there is no common language, but that the two are using the same language with different understandings. For instance, there is the common term, "love." Everybody knows what love means, or do they?

In the quotation above, St Paul aimed to convey to his spiritual children in Corinth "the most perfect way" to follow the Lord and thereby fulfill one's life. He thought of all a Christian might strive for in a lifetime, then he topped the list with love. He felt the best case for love's priority over all the other gifts with which the Holy Spirit blesses us is that love will never be terminated. Even faith and hope, as essential as they are to a life in Christ on earth, one day will pass from our existence, while the love we practice here on earth will follow us into the Father's Kingdom. It's not just that our deeds of love will be tallied up on the great scorecard in Heaven, but even more important, each time we demonstrate an act of pure, selfless, loving concern for another human, an animal, or a plant, we identify ourselves with the Creator. Simply stated, we become ourselves godlike in our willingness to sacrifice our private selves for the well-being of another living thing. That kind of love will never be outdated. The same character trait will be required in God's Kingdom.

But love in the popular meaning—mere sexual relations, together with all the emotions that precede or follow what is called "making love"—holds no promise of an eternally lasting relationship. In fact, most popular songs tend to admire love for its brevity, as though that itself made it more appealing. We have become conditioned to expect little more from love, since that is the message presented in songs and art forms. Some of the silliest ideas pass for wisdom when put to music. For example, the lyrics of a French pop song that became a hit in the United States are: "but if you stay, I'll make you a day like no other day and no other way . . . 'ne me quitte pas' don't go away."

The obvious reply to such a proposal should be: "But what of tomorrow? Or next week, or next year, for that matter?" Should we think about our lives for more than a day at a time, or is the lover so egotistical that he feels one "day" of love should be enough to last forever? Sexual love reaches a climax, then wanes. Nothing transcends the moment. It can only be repeated, like any other human appetite. There is nothing beyond the act itself, but we are created to live not only a lifetime, but forever. The way we spend our days here on earth distinctively affects the life everlasting that awaits us beyond the grave.

If it were only emotional nonsense we might pass it off as teenage sentimentality, but we all know that here is the cause of so many divorces in our society. Not all, certainly, but many marriages are broken by the inability of the couple to move on from mere sexuality to further aspects of love, such as caring for one another, taking responsibility for the family, suffering with one another's problems, and learning to suppress one's own desires for the sake of somebody else. These are examples of a lifetime of standing in love, just as in the Orthodox sacrament of marriage the man and woman are led forward to stand together with crowns on their heads, being made to realize that even in that physical manner they must remain standing upright always, or the crowns will fall from their heads. The point is obvious; "falling" in love is rather simple to do and a whole lot of fun, but to stand in love, and to keep on standing, returning to one's feet after every blow this world inflicts on a couple, is noble, heroic, and nothing less than what Christ expects of those who say they know what love is all about, and who seek to practice loving for more than a lifetime.

30
Endless Love

Love never ends. As for prophecies, they will pass away; as for tongues, they will cease; as for knowledge, it will pass away.
(1 Corinthians 13:8)

When a missionary sets out to take the gospel to a people, he first researches the attitudes and beliefs, the presuppositions and mind-sets of those he wishes to influence. St Paul understood the Hellenistic principles underlying the educational system of the times, and he realized that the Greeks of Corinth would set a high value on that which is eternal.

For them, anything that truly exists lasts forever. All else is merely accidental and subject to change; it is in a state of flux, altering in form and mass, depending on time and conditions as it searches for its true essence, when all will come to a state of rest and harmony.

As new Christians, the Corinthians were eager to grow spiritually—so eager, in fact, that they competed with one another for the spiritual gifts that affirm their sanctity. That competition reflected a lack of love. To impress upon them the significance of love, indeed, to make it clear that love must always lead the list of virtues or else the other gifts of the Spirit would be of little avail, he pointed out the eternal nature of love.

Everything else will pass away with time. Who would

not treasure the ability to predict what is to happen in the future? Not by the pseudo-science of astrology or mere calculated speculation, but by a clear vision of the plan of God for what will be. But once the forecast is realized in history, what value is the prediction?

If one is able to speak several languages of humanity, even that ability will be of little use when Christ returns and makes this world's methods of communication obsolete, for those of God's Kingdom will require no translators or interpreters. If, on the other hand, St Paul here means glossolalia, speaking (or babbling) in the Spirit, that also will be transcended in the Second Coming.

Who does not enjoy the excitement of learning; yet, knowledge of things on earth will be superceded by the unity of the believer with divinity, for our knowledge is only conditional, fit for time and history, added together piece by piece or, rather, by referring one sense impression to an earlier one, ever correcting, modifying, or adjusting. Then, however, all will become instantly and totally clear to us, without the need to ponder or ruminate.

Love, only love will last forever. Every instance of self-giving love is being recorded for eternity; but even more, it is affirming and continuing the process of transforming the lover into what he is to be, and in some sense is already, in Heaven.

Does that quality of endlessness speak to the heart of a modern person? Does it matter in a throw-away culture that only one form of relationship will leave an indelible impression on his being? Long after the last cosmic star is no more, an act of self-giving love will be remembered and imbedded in the soul of its agent. Does that make any sense to a creature who has been conditioned to value little more than physical well-being, economic security, material prosperity, and social respectability? How does such a person appreciate the thrust of Paul's words regarding the durability of love?

Yet the Greeks who could contemplate eternal beauty in a statue, who conceived the ideal form of things, who considered a harmony of shapes that would not submit to collapse or confusion, had an instinctive feel for the eternal aspect of love. What might it mean for a person today, for whom love mostly begins with an urge and moves through flirtation to spasm, if he were told that the greatest attribute of love is not excitement or repetition, not even the feeling it brings within, but the truth that it lives forever in the mind of God and in the soul of the sacrificial lover?

31
Fit for the Kingdom

For we know in part, and we prophesy in part.
(1 Corinthians 13:9)

One might think that we today, living through the last years of the second millennium since Christ, would comprehend the truth of these words more readily than those living in any era before us. Must we be told that we understand things imperfectly, we who were told in school that mathematics is pure science, that one either knows it or doesn't, only to discover that in the past few years the computer phenomenon has made us return to the classroom and relearn all we thought we knew all these years?

By means of technological advances based on scientific discoveries we can discern something of what future generations will experience. We base our "prophecies" on the information we have at hand, though we realize we shall not be on earth to experience the life in that future. But the holy apostle is speaking not of a future life on earth that a contemporary generation will not be around to enjoy. Rather, he is referring to a life in God's Kingdom to which we all have a clear invitation.

"We know in part." First, the fact is that our knowledge is only temporary, and that itself is a prodigious insight. We know, for instance, that the values that apply in this life will be obsolete in the Kingdom. Here it is the "survival of the fittest." There, compassion will be revered. Here, self-promoters who have no hesitation to shove others aside seem to prevail. There, the "last shall be first." Here, "the squeaky wheel gets oiled." There, the meek receive the Lord's inheritance.

When we read the gospel we are presented with an example of proper behavior for the future Kingdom of Heaven by Jesus Himself, and an example of the manner He relates to persons and situations. He shows us what is expected if we are to become like Him. If we develop as God's adopted children, love will be the measure of all our relationships. Because we have come to know Jesus, we have both an understanding and a model of what we ourselves ought to be like.

Charles Darwin, the man credited with teaching the world that human life began with the animals, himself found how difficult it was to teach virtue to a savage. Returning from the Pacific Islands where he conceived his famous theory of evolution, he took a young cannibal on his trip back to England. There, he taught him the ways of civilized humanity, how to read and write, the way to dress, eat, and behave in an advanced society. The native returned to his own land. Later, when an expedition from England had been overcome and slaughtered by a band of savages, it was discovered that their leader was the very same person who had been "educated and refined" in England.

Likewise, it will not be enough to be admitted into Heaven if our hearts and souls have not become radically changed. If the Lord is truly all-knowing, how could He possibly tolerate somebody with the soul of a savage? If we in this lifetime can do little better than strike back at our attacker, always insisting on our own way, demanding that we be heard and provided for, how will that behavioral pattern prepare us for the person we are called to be in God's Holy Kingdom? If at each liturgy we sing of the blessings those receive who are merciful, meek, and pure in heart, who are persecuted for doing good and reviled for upholding Christ's values, what shall we reply when it is pointed out that we had lived out our lives "just like everybody else," which is to say that we had been as hard and intolerant, greedy and envious, impatient and angry as the normal people around us? Darwin's savage may have worn creased trousers and polished shoes, but that alone didn't make a gentle gentleman. We also may sing hymns of praise to God and receive the Holy Communion regularly, but if our hearts are not becoming ever more like the heart of Jesus, we are only natives of this world, and not yet citizens of the Kingdom.

32
Life's Transitions

When I was a child I talked like a child, I spoke like a child, I thought like a child, I reasoned like a child. When I became a man, I put childish ways behind me.
(1 Corinthians 13:11)

When we think of life in the Kingdom of God, if we do at all, we accept the blandest, most shop-worn ideas on the subject. One hears well-intentioned Christians say that we shall all become angels. Wrong. Angels are another category in God's Kingdom entirely. As beings bereft of bodies they are pure spirits without the complexities of human beings. Others will say that at death we divide into body and soul. The body is then sloughed off, presumably like the booster rockets that propel the space ships beyond the earth's field of gravity, only to fall uselessly to the earth while the "soul" continues on its journey into the outer reaches of the cosmos. Not so. A soulless body is only a corpse, nothing more, while a bodiless soul is merely a ghost. A phantom. A spook. Whatever our souls will be like in God's Kingdom, they will be mystically joined together with a body, our body, so that we shall maintain and complete our integrity of personhood, like Christ Jesus who made clear to His disciples after His resurrection that He was more than a ghost or an apparition: "A ghost does not have flesh and bones, as you see I have" (Lk 24:39).

Although St Paul states that we cannot know everything about God's Kingdom because our frame of reference is limited, he did not suggest that we ought not to think about the subject. Because we cannot learn everything, that does not mean we are to give up trying to discover all we can about life everlasting. He draws the analogy from childhood, with which every adult can readily relate.

The child's world is filled with wonder and fantasy. Adults are beyond a child's control, and therefore may be considered beyond reasoning as well, while inanimate objects can be brought to life with a bit of imagination. As children we can be anything we wish to be; we only have to use our talent for make-believe. No matter how drab and sordid the daily routine, regardless of the grownups that clutter the world with their inconsistent demands on little folk, children can separate themselves from their so-called "real" world and climb up into the secret place of their own realities, which they insist is only make-believe.

Then one day they grow up. They take their places in the world of adults and without realizing it, the grown-up world becomes their own. The realm of fairy tales and wonder closes itself, as in the song: "Once you pass its portals, you may never return again."

The problem for most of us is that we stop here. We take for granted that this adult world is the only existence possible. Jesus said, "In my father's house there are many mansions. If it were not so, would I have told you that I go to prepare a place for you?" (Jn 14:2).

Even the shallowest Christian would not deny that life exists beyond the grave. But that life is not a mere consolation prize for those unfortunate enough to die—it is the goal for which this life is merely a preparation. This state of existence only makes sense in that light. Otherwise, this world is a macabre, hollow joke. How dreadful, that we should journey through this world, ever learning, ever weighing, ever assimilating and evaluating each experience that confronts us, discovering whom we can trust and whom to avoid, learning how to deal with temptations, what to value, and what in the end only brings grief to our lives—in a word, to complete the university curriculum of this world after having paid the expensive tuition costs in suffering—just to have it all placed in a coffin and lowered into the grave. If the world makes sense at all, what is the reason behind such a plan, and what kind of God would have arranged it that way?

We Christians believe that this is not the case at all; yet, if that is so, why are we so hesitant to think of, to anticipate, and to imagine our lives as they will be eventually lived with Christ in the Father's Kingdom? Are we so involved with existing in this world that we prefer to ignore what lies ahead? Then indeed we are living as though this world were preferable to the next. Are we in fact spiritual cowards, frightened by the journey we will assuredly all take? Then we have not only little faith, but we have not a great deal of love either, since "perfect love casts out all fear" (1 Jn 4:18).

How far this civilization has come from merely a few generations ago, when Charles Dickens was able to summarize his novel with the justification for living that all would grasp immediately, when he put on his hero's lips the following words, just as he was about to be hanged: "It is a far, far better rest that I go to, than I have known" (*A Tale of Two Cities*). How many, we wonder, would say the same in our own time?

33
The Icon in the Mirror

Now we see in a mirror indistinctly, but then we shall see face to face.
(1 Corinthians 13:12)

Mirrors are everywhere, nobody ignores them. Toddlers play peekaboo with themselves, teenagers probe for blemishes or almost incessantly comb their hair, the middle-aged measure their stomach overflow or search for grey hair and wrinkles. All these are reflected dutifully and clearly in the mirror. St Paul's mirror returns an unclear image, one, however, worthy of a meditation. Commentaries point to the poor quality of mirrors in his day; they were little more than polished metal surfaces, much inferior to contemporary standards. But this does not cancel the thrust of his intention.

Precisely because we see ourselves so well, we fail to look harder at our true image. The surface reflection is only skin deep. We must explore ourselves beneath the superficial—complexion, hairline, muscle tone, dress, and the like. The base image of our inner selves lies deeper than what appears to our sight.

People of the past understood this probably better than we do today; at least they sought to discern who they were by engaging insightful portrait painters to reveal what they perceived of their personalities. The great painters of the past explored those they were about to paint, striving to capture not only surface impressions, but the character of their subjects. Properly conceptualized and transmitted to canvas, the discerning viewer would then recognize something of the essence of the subject that transcends the elements of time. The person portrayed in the same way will realize his innermost being; the traits he may try to disguise from the world, and even from himself, cannot be hid. If the artist is skillful and thorough, he may even expose family traits which pass from one generation to the next, and the idiosyncrasies of behavior that work their way through each member of a family.

Even without paintings, we frequently mark in a youngster's attitudes and behavioral patterns the characteristics that follow him through life and mold his personality. We think we know others quite well, and in a sense that is correct, because we look at others as objects outside ourselves, and in that way we are literally objective, even to those dearest to us. Looking in a mirror, on the other hand, is to stare at ourselves. Others know us from outside, but only we know what lies within. They can be helpful in revealing what we appear to be like to the outside world, but they know only the exterior and they judge us by our overt behavior.

St Paul refers to self-awareness. This is what he means by seeing "indistinctly." He is calling on us to search for what God sees in us. Put another way, if we were made in the "Image of God" (Gn 1:26), what must that image look like?

Surely it cannot be identified with the self that is constantly changing through the years of this world's life; at least, it cannot be the same as what is constantly passing, since God is without change. It goes without saying that the Image of God cannot be enhanced by cosmetic make-up and dyes that are used to hold back aging and unattractiveness.

If God is love, and we were made in His Image, then

we were made to love, and when we love we are most like God. Be sure, however, that we always make the distinction of spiritual love, which includes compassion, tenderness, concern for others, service, goodness, gentleness, forgiveness, and understanding. It has little to do with the erotic love this world cares most about. Eroticism is a display of affection in order to satisfy one's own needs, not for the well-being of the other. Erotic love looks in the mirror and sees a surface reflection. *Agape,* that form of love which is more concerned with the other's happiness than one's own, searches for the true person deep inside the outward impression. Erotic love cares for the appearance of the moment; agape builds up what will never end. Spiritual, agape love glows from within the heart. It can be recognized in the icons of the Orthodox Church.

Icons are those images that manifest the human being filled with the Holy Spirit, radiating that Spirit from deep inside, while reflecting the Lord's Image. This is the meaning of the apostle's words, "face to face." The God in us looks upon the God who is not only here or there, but everywhere, and this brings forth an identification. It does not mean that we lose our personalities in the process of loving, as though we were somehow blended into the essence of the godhead, but on the contrary, we discover who we truly are, who it was that God made when He created us, and what we are intended to be when we are filled with agape love, which manifests the Image of God in our beings.

34
The Judgment of Love

Then we shall see face to face . . . Then I shall understand fully, even as I have been understood.
(1 Corinthians 13:12)

To come face to face with the Lord is to see God—an overwhelming thought—and to be seen by Him. It means that we will be judged for what we are—certainly with love, yet openly and truthfully. All that we have accomplished and everything that we have failed to achieve will be exposed with His searching, all-knowing eyes. Our score of failures and successes will be made apparent in an instant.

The non-Christian might ask why we should be judged at all. If God made us creatures possessing some dignity, then He might just as well respect our "right" to privacy and self-esteem, rather than expose to heaven's inhabitants all that we are and have achieved or failed to accomplish. At least two responses are in order:

First, to assume that our deeds and lives are unknown to all who are in the Holy Spirit is a form of spiritual blindness. If we are just beginning to learn the way computers are able to keep track of our habits and bring forth instantaneously our past record, if we are only starting to discover ways to make sensitive devices that can determine our present physical condition by revealing the evidence of our past illnesses and their damage to our organs, how naive it is to underestimate the Lord's ability to know every detail of what we have done and shall ever do in this world or the next.

Second, to judge us is a way of respecting our persons and our potential for virtue. Ours is a society that sets standards for behavior, just as every society does. In fact, we make assumptions for human beings based upon their inner sense of goodness. We expect a person to enhance life and to avoid whatever brings pain or injury to any living creature. If a person should do otherwise and is incapable of realizing his errors, we eventually treat him in a special way. We label such a person abnormal, and he is separated from society at large. No longer is he to be judged by the standards of conventional behavior.

When the Church invites us to make frequent confessions, it does so because this is the way to conduct intermediate judgments on ourselves with the help of an objective, compassionate, and understanding guide. These are checkups on the pathway to the Kingdom of God, opportunities for us to try discerning what the Lord knows as He looks at us at a moment in time, as we progress through our lifetime. Looking at icons in the proper way will also provide reflections of our inner state, so that we might measure our spiritual soundness by the wholesome goodness that comes to us from the faces of Jesus and the saints. These judgments are not to be resented or ignored, but welcomed.

Would an athlete who is seriously intent on qualifying for Olympic competition resent having his speed timed against a stopwatch? Rather, he should welcome the information it provides about the progress he is making, and apply the information accordingly. So, also, if we are intent upon becoming one of those who are among the family of Christ, we must be serious about matching the records of the elect of God, welcoming the observations of our lives that will teach us how we are growing on the way toward accomplishing the will of the Lord through our lives.

35
To Love Him is to Know Him

Now I know in part; then I shall know completely.
(1 Corinthians 13:12)

The greater part of the educational process is not to fill a student with facts, but to reveal an awareness of the vast unknown. To awaken the quest for knowledge requires a certain insight: I do not know—I wish to know—I shall not be satisfied until I know all that is possible to comprehend, regardless of the cost.

Some, not all of us, discover in childhood that the truth about knowledge is precisely the reverse of the common attitude. What passes for knowledge or even wisdom to simple people turns out to be mere opinion, instant analysis on any and every subject imaginable. The glib, slick, quick talker exposes himself as shallow in the final accounting, an entertainer of those who have never acquired a taste for profundity. In fact, intelligence may be measured by the ability to resist the temptation to appease oneself with a premature resolution to a problem that requires long, intensive deliberation.

To realize, like St Paul, that "now I know in part" is already an achievement. And to comprehend that by the very nature of things partial comprehension will be the condition of our life in this world opens us to ponder and decide how to apply that awareness of our incomplete knowledge.

Is it a matter of time alone? If so, we could do nothing

but wait for the Kingdom and be satisfied to know not a whole lot until Christ's glorious return. But if He is the Lord of time, and if it is true that in Him the future can invade our present time, as appears to be the case when Christ took three apostles to reveal creation as God intended in the Transfiguration, we realize that our knowledge of truth can be expanded—not only can it be, but the Lord Himself desires us to know more about Him.

One handicap is that we tend to think of knowledge as though it has to do with our minds alone. It's a Western way of thinking, foreign to Eastern Christians, yet it infects us with wrong attitudes, as though we were becoming so clever that we were discovering God's hidden secrets and in a way exposing His awesome powers, which makes God unhappy.

The Orthodox approach, which is the only true approach to learning, is certainly not to avoid thinking and take everything purely on faith—God gave us minds to think with—but to know that knowledge is more than a mental process. Our heart and spirit must share in the experience. When we say we "comprehend" we already imply a total, wholistic awareness.

Simply put, our minds cannot know if our bodies are in sin; or, put better, our souls and bodies interact. Light has nothing to do with darkness and "if the light within you is darkness, how great is that darkness," as Christ said (Mt 6:23). One must be pure to really comprehend the deep things of God. Fasting, prayer, and contemplation are elements in the learning process, because we are integral beings, functioning wholistically. To people without the blessing of spiritual insight, this will appear as nonsense, for they are limited to intellectual knowledge, devoid of unity with the grace that pours forth from God (although this too comes from divinity, as everything in the universe). Still, to know is to grow ever more in the direction of the source of all knowledge, the Holy Trinity who, far from wanting us to wallow in ignorance, sent the world the Living Word, Christ Jesus, who is ever meeting our inadequate knowledge with the fullness of truth, light, wisdom, and knowledge as we prepare ourselves to receive it.

In profound simplicity, to love the Lord is to know Him, and we cannot know Him unless we love Him, which requires making ourselves ready both to love and to know by cleansing ourselves from sin through prayer, meditation, fasting, Bible study, and imitation of the holy saints who lived their lives in a process of learning ever more about the God of love and wisdom.

36
Now and Then

For now we see in a mirror dimly, but then face to face. Now I know in part; then I shall understand fully, even as I have been fully understood.
(1 Corinthians 13:12)

The heart of the gospel's message is the transition from this world to the Kingdom of God. In order to comprehend St Paul's message one must separate time into:

a. the present, which is the moment of opportunity to prepare oneself and anybody who will follow Christ, and

b. the future time, which is not merely time that has not happened, but the unmeasurable, the timeless state of being in God's realm, where everything is subject to infinity.

Notice how the apostle ends the love story in the thirteenth chapter of 1 Corinthians. Two verses speak of "now" and "then." Now we see obscurely as though gazing into a defective mirror where the reflection is not quite clear, but then we shall see directly, "face to face." Now I comprehend only partially, and if I am truly wise I realize how little knowledge I have in relation to all it is possible to know about the universe of God, its component parts, and the Creator's intention for it all, especially for myself; but then I shall know completely all that I have been surmising and gleaning from hints left in the universe by the Creator.

To live on earth in this time frame is not natural, but this cannot deter us. It requires a gift from the Holy Spirit, and that gift, grace, is always subject to being withdrawn if we choose to abandon our life in the Spirit and revert to a life reduced to the flesh, and to the logic of this world.

Living in constant preparation for the coming Kingdom, we will be judged by this world as dishonoring the world by those who can see only a material existence. Of course the true Christian will reply that no greater honor can be given to this world than to restore it to its original intention. That which is natural to this world is inadequate to what God had in mind when He created it. For instance, it is natural for the human being to die; therefore, from the world's point of view a man only frustrates himself by resisting the inevitability of death. He should free himself from the wish to survive death, which is illusory, and find peace in surrendering to extinction.

We Christians would say that the very desire for life beyond death, the resistance to extinction, is an affirmation of the original plan of God that we all should live with Him here in this world, and in the next. Wisdom, for the secular humanist, just as for the Stoics who preceded him, lies in the "knowledge" that life terminates in death. Wisdom for the Christian lies in the certainty that this life is merely a foretaste of the life to come. It is as though we were at the performance of an opera. We take our seats, the curtain is closed, the orchestra begins to play. They sound various themes that will be expanded and given fuller meaning in the drama that is to come. Hints and allusions are all we receive. The curtain does not open, however, in this artwork of life. All that is yet to be revealed will be presented to us only beyond the grave.

But life *now* is more than merely sitting passively in the

audience, staring ahead at a closed curtain. Preparing for God's Kingdom calls for an ongoing transformation of ourselves, divesting our beings of the values that will not follow us beyond our death, and assimilating the virtues that will make us fit to live with Christ in His Father's realm. Before we do that, we must first be thoroughly convinced that the Bible is correct in announcing God's Kingdom, and we have to commit ourselves irrevocably to living now for the life then, or we shall hopelessly, helplessly flounder somewhere between two contradictory viewpoints of life. Each human being must reply for himself to the challenge put by the prophet Elijah ages ago: "How long will you waver between two opinions? If God is God, then follow Him . . ." (1 Kgs 18:21).

37
Love's Company

So there remain faith, hope, and love.
(1 Corinthians 13:13)

Always they are united, that trinity of virtues, and we think of them together. In fact the verb "remain" is singular in Greek, all the more binding them into a unity. They together accompany us through the pilgrimage of Christian living that begins at our baptism. All of them aim us toward the future that is awaiting us.

Faith is not belief in something, an idea or a plan for the universe that makes sense, but rather a total trust in one God, whose ways are often hidden from our reason, yet whose will we affirm as long as we continue receiving grace to believe in that plan which is still being worked out despite the negative elements of history—this century of wars, upheavals, and sufferings brought to living things, including misery, pain, and death as well as the ongoing fear of annihilation by nuclear armaments. The same God who revealed Himself in Jesus Christ as Alpha, the Beginning, is also the Omega, the last letter of the last word of history. And He is speaking now to those whose ears are listening and obeying.

Hope grants us the energy that continues our progress through time. Hope is the dance of life that inspires and encourages us, smiling when we are glum or too serious, the forefinger that curls under the chin and lifts our crestfallen heads to look up and see the way ahead. Faith confirms the God in whom we believe; hope leads us toward Him.

But without love we can lose both faith and hope. Hate is a constant reminder of wrongs and injuries suffered, a memory that binds us to the past and prevents our advance. We eventually lose our vision of unity with Christ who is ever out ahead of us, and instead become obsessed with the need for revenge or else, more passively, we become frozen in the state of loveless apathy. In either case, faith flees from us, for we no longer trust in God's plan. We say to ourselves: did He not fail to exact revenge on the one who harmed us? And hope turns to despair, since we fail to recognize any change taking place, expecting and even insisting that the world should conform to our plan for it, rather than converting ourselves to an ever new awareness of God's plan at work in the universe and within ourselves. Somebody who is in the death grip of hatred will never be free of the past as long as he insists on hating, because only love can release him to the future.

It is truly surprising that many persons fail to understand the compelling logic of this human experience. If only they could, it would clarify the mystery we have regarding life after death.

St Paul says that only love lasts. Faith will no longer be necessary when we are brought before the object of our faith, the Lord of glory, when hope will be vindicated, because the future will evolve into an eternal present; but love will be always fresh and bright. To love is to be like God, for it is to love as He loves, and to love what He loves.

Like the mother who would never conceive of measuring the hugs and fondlings she pours out upon her infant in order to seek an equal recompense in later years, but who rather counts the pleasure of loving as life's greatest delight, so love like God's love is unstinting, without a requirement. To live in eternal joy one must become godlike in the sense of loving, always loving, and loving everything that God loves. Not to do so is to be in hell, which is not a place, but a condition:

the accursed affliction of hate, a cancer of the soul that tortures not so much the object of one's anger and bitterness, but the subject.

38
The Priority of Love

In this life we have three great lasting qualities—faith, hope, and love. *(1 Corinthians 13:13)*

Those three awesome gifts come to us in the very order in which they are presented. Vladimir Lossky put it this way:

> One can say equally well, that the Old Testament lived by faith, and moved toward hope; that the age of the Gospel lives in hope and moves toward love; that love is a mystery which will only be fully revealed and realized in the age to come. (*Mystical Theology of the Eastern Church* [Crestwood, NY: St Vladimir's Seminary Press, 1976] p. 232)

Faith is like the winter season, when we are confident that the earth under the snow contains the seeds of beautiful flowers and fruitful plants, and we trust that life will be renewed once again. Hope comes with the springtime, for the blossoms and buds assure us that there will be a harvest of plenty; not a guarantee, certainly, since many dangers may prevent a bumper crop—drought, locusts, frost, hurricanes. Still, we live in expectation that blessings will abound.

But love is for every season and hour, both of this life and the life to come. Love is never wrong. In the winter of our darkest times, when we are held fast in the bonds of depression, self-pity, and remorse, when we have lost trust in everybody and every plan, even our own, at a time when we no longer have a burning faith in God because we have lost faith in ourselves, even then if we are able to find love in our hearts for some other living thing, we may find a way out of the gloom and into the light once again. This is why animals, birds, even a rodent or an insect is able to generate a concern for something other than our own misery in the souls of prisoners, the mentally ill, and the retarded.

Love is important in our happy times as well, when we are filled with hope that we shall prosper and that everything is going our way; indeed, without love we can readily become selfish and insensitive to the real needs of others around us who are not so well off as we. This is why it is so difficult for wealthy people to enter the Kingdom of Heaven. They have a hard time loving, because they feel others simply want a share of the material goods they have in abundance.

Part of the mystery of love is that there is nothing utilitarian about it; that is, it will not help our striving to succeed in this life if we are so filled with ambition that we walk ruthlessly over anybody in our way toward that great idol, success. Those who arrive there inform the rest of us that it is a lonely place at the top. And no wonder. They have paid a dear price in the currency of love.

The cross of Christ is a symbol of all that is opposite to worldly success. As we meditate on the cross we would do well to consider the mystery of love that it manifests: the love of the Father for the world, despite its unworthiness and its inability to fathom, much less return, that love; the love of the Son, to submit Himself to the will of the Father regardless of the shame, pain, agony, and rejection which the cross entailed; the love of the Holy Spirit for us, shown by patiently waiting around and within us for the opportunity to lead us to greater epiphanies of God's love for us, as we grow in the capacity to receive such profound revelations.

39
Christian Charity

Follow after charity. (1 Corinthians 14:1 KJV)

Charity, as defined in Webster's Collegiate Dictionary, comes from the Latin for "dear, or loved": *caras.* Its meanings include: 1. Christian love: specifically, (a) (now rare) Divine love for man, (b) Act of loving all men as brothers because they are sons of God; 2. An act of feeling affection or benevolence; 3. Good will to the poor and the suffering; almsgiving; also, alms; hence, public provision for the relief of the poor.

Instructive, is it not, that "charity" is something specifically Christian? Critics quite frequently disagree, and indeed it is not difficult to demonstrate that those nations converted to Christianity were not always able to rise to the lofty ideals of justice for all, including the weak and powerless, to righteousness mitigated by mercy, and compassion set forth in legislation based on the gospel; yet those who criticize do so by the very Christian standards introduced by the teachings of Christ.

The reforms of Constantine the Great manifested a gentleness in every legislation that dealt with women, children, orphans, dependents, and slaves. After his victory over his adversary, Licinius, Constantine moved swiftly to alter the laws of the Roman Empire to hold in higher regard the attitude toward the family, procuring new rights for wives and children.

Charity as an ongoing, substantial care for the poor was proclaimed by St John Chrysostom. He stated that where we say our daily prayers is not just where we keep our prayer book and Bible. There should be also a container for our daily contributions for the needy. How odd to our modern ears to hear that prayer is a great privilege which is not to be presumed or taken for granted. In order to show our gratitude to the Holy Trinity for listening to our prayer, we ought to take into account all living things in God's blessed creation who are also in need of His grace. That is, we should not pray caring for only our personal needs, but as creatures caring for everybody and all that lives, aware of others who are at that very moment torn with pains of hunger, thirst, confusion, cold, sickness, shame, grief, self-hatred, or bitterness who are more than we in need of the Lord's tender love and healing mercy. True Christians were always more concerned for the needs of others than for their own. They searched for ways to help others in direct, meaningful acts of charity, and not merely with their sympathy and prayers.

Another instance of charity comes to mind. A young man who had been coopted into the Roman military ranks was on maneuvers in northern Africa. He noticed that there was a group of civilians, simple folk who at great personal risk to themselves had been caring for the needs of prisoners captured by the Roman legion. Curious about their intentions he inquired about them. He was told that they were the followers of a certain Jesus whom they claimed was the savior of the world. When his term of service ended, the man returned to the area where he first met the Christians. He sought them out, learned their teachings and received baptism. That former soldier, Pachomius, lived as a hermit in the desert. Later he assembled a community of men like himself who chose to live apart from society, thus becoming the founder of communal monasticism—all because his curious eye noticed those people called Christians who acted in an unusual manner, in a world of people who only behave in ways that help themselves.

Here is an excerpt from a letter titled "A Charge to My Children," written at the dawn of Christianity in Russia by Vladimir Monomakh:

> My children, praise God and love men. . . . Forget not the poor, but feed them. Remember that riches come from God and are given to you for only a brief time. . . . Be fathers to orphans, be judges in widows' causes, and do not permit the powerful to oppress the weak. Do not put to death either the innocent or the guilty, for nothing is as sacred as the life and soul of a Christian. Do not desert the sick. . . .

III. FROM OTHER PARTS OF THE BIBLE

40
The Tear Wiper

And the Lord God will wipe away tears from all faces.
(Isaiah 25:8)

Is it any wonder the prophecy of Isaiah sometimes is termed the fifth gospel, although it had been written hundreds of years before the coming in the flesh of our Lord and Savior, Jesus Christ? Its insight into the nature of the Lord God Almighty, so frequently presented in the Old Testament as a stern God, punishing His people for breaking the covenant and falling away into sin—that same God is revealed by Isaiah as He who will "wipe away tears from all faces."

When we attempt an estimate of the tears shed throughout the course of humanity's history on earth, we are stymied. What a melancholy meditation—would all those tears fill a lake? No doubt. Which one? Perhaps the Great Salt Lake in Utah; better, the Dead Sea of the Holy Land, both of which are bitter from the amount of saline compound in them. Tears are like that, too. To count the many tears of all humanity we should revert to using the term "googol," which is the figure 1 followed by one hundred zeroes. It looks like this: 100000000000000000000000000000000000000000000000000000 00000000000000000000000000000000000000000000000. Overwhelming, yet we are told and we are sure that God is aware of every tear that ever was shed from every eye He ever made. And He will wipe away each tear. No human emotion has ever been unnoticed by Him, no suffering has ever escaped His attention, no sigh has ever not been heard.

The passage from Isaiah is all the more forceful because of the image it conjures up in our imagination. It is the concerned parent who the child knows from previous experience is compassionate and full of understanding, who will kneel before us to be on our level to communicate more easily or, even better, swoop up the child in strong arms, holding tightly the loved one in a secure embrace until the trembling upsetting him subsides. Purposely we use the general term parent, rather than to specify which one, since compassion is truly sexless. We presently are undergoing a period of apparent conflict between some women and some men over their roles in society. Perhaps it was the case in the United States that masculinity implied scorn for basic emotions and femininity provided solace and comfort to those in need of affection and understanding, but we might take a clue from the holy Scriptures.

God is the Heavenly Father, Son, and Holy Spirit, the Creator and Sustainer of the universe, the Almighty Judge who is at the same time the "Wiper of Tears" from every human eye. Compassionate Judge, yet Righteous Comforter. We humans have assumed it is best for a child, or at least the more natural, to be raised by a firm, authoritarian father and a gentle, understanding mother; however, the total person ought to be both firm and gentle, disciplined and compassionate. It is not a matter of gender or of roles, but of completeness as a human being.

Elsewhere in the Church we have an insight related to this basic point. Listen to the holy Gospel read on certain feast days in honor of the blessed Mother of God and ever virgin Mary (Lk 10:38-42). It is the story of the friends of Jesus and sisters of Lazarus, Martha and Mary. Martha was a purposeful, self-disciplined, outspoken, no-nonsense leader, much like St Peter, who liked to get things done. Mary was quiet, gentle, humble, filled with compassion for all living things. The other

Mary, the mother of Jesus, who is for all Christians a prototype of the ideal person, not only for women but for men also, was a combination of the best qualities of both sisters: meek yet decisive, understanding yet stern with herself in fulfilling to her utmost capacity the will of God in her life. She transcends the limits we moderns set—types, we call them: introverts and extroverts, ectomorphs and endomorphs. Does it matter, when suffering is thrust upon us, what type of person we are, whether we cry openly and unabashedly or suppress our tears, reacting with anger and rage instead? The tears are there, dripping slowly from our hearts.

And He knows of them as well. God senses our tears and acknowledges them. How hard it must be to be God, knowing what He alone comprehends, the causes and continuations of our anguish, the plumpness of each tear. And He answers by a promise that He will wipe away every one of them. He who planned only happiness and songs must look upon all of our self-inflicted agonies and dirges. So let us then cry, knowing that this is the way to be in touch with our deepest emotions, accounting for the sufferings within us. God will not keep us from crying, nor will He ridicule our weeping as infantile, unworthy of proper behavior for a Christian; He will not only then in His Kingdom, but even now, when we ask Him, wipe away our tears so that we not remain in our grief and make misery a way of life that leads to continual self-pity, feelings of frustration, and an inability to cope with the realities of existence, becoming perpetual hand-wringers who are ever exuding a spirit of pessimism and a defeatist attitude in every situation.

No, our God is filled with love and concern for our well-being, caring for us as a perfect parent, comforting us in order that we may take up the daily task of courageously fulfilling His will in the world that is placed in our control.

41
Your Heart as a Gift

My son, give me your heart.
(Proverbs 23:26)

The Lord wants nothing less than your heart. Very well, you respond, He may have it when you are through using it. Let it be for now the muscle pumping vital blood through your body. But it is more than a mere muscle. The Bible informs us that the heart is the place where all of our feelings come together, where our emotions reside, the center of our deepest personality. Poets and songwriters who put heart and soul together have the right concept. The heart is where we have our deepest and most lasting experiences. In the heart is where we meet God. Put another way, if what truly exists within us is the part that will endure and continue after this brief life is ended, and if that part which we sometimes call soul can be located in the heart, then the heart is everything.

As modern persons influenced by western civilization we should, all of us who have been educated in the schools of our culture, think of the mind as the locus of our emotions, and the body as a mechanism. But somebody coming from a truly Eastern Christian culture will have a reverence for the heart that is uncommon to westerners. This insight came to me in a discussion in Crete with a Greek cardiologist who had studied the heart's workings in the greatest institutions of the world, who yet felt that the spiritual aspects of the most vital human organ made it much more than the body's pump.

"Give me your heart," the Lord requests. Other parts of our bodies concern us intensely. How many agonize over the shape of the nose—too long, broken, extremely crooked, or just pug. A person, especially teenagers, may be too tall and gangly or too short. She or he may be plagued with acne, oily skin, pock marks, or blemishes. He may be overweight, homely, or handicapped in some way. Those elements of our bodies matter greatly and influence the way we reach out to others for communion. But as important as they are at a given period of life, in the long run our hearts are sought by the Lord.

When He wants your heart is not after you are through with it. He wants it now, but not as it is. He desires rather that you commit yourself to surrendering your heart to Him at this very moment, then go through the remaining time of your life cleansing, shining, preparing it further for the time when He will come to claim it.

Think of your heart as a gift you are giving to God. What condition is it in? Is it full of uncontrolled rage, ready to erupt at the slightest tiny provocation? What will He do with a spiritually defective heart? Is it encrusted with images of lewd, vulgar, debasing, immoral acts? Is this what you are preparing as a gift to present to your Creator? Is it sopping and dripping with self-pity, remembered injuries, and scars of unforgiveness? Is it a cowardly heart that has never faced up to a challenge, never spoken out for the values of the Gospel and the teachings of Christ, but rather shrivels up whenever the beasts of the world attack?

You will cleanse and purify it, you decide. You will fill it with peace, thoughts of harmony and prayer, joy and love. Can you do it alone? You need not even try, for the Lord who seeks your heart wishes to come into your heart and to share it with you. Before He can claim it, He must have your approval. When He made us, He gave us the freedom to elect whether we wish to live in unity with Him, or to live apart from His grace and precious presence. He will come and live in your heart, blessing all that is really you, which He created you to become; but you alone must sincerely, completely, and irrevocably entrust your heart and your whole being to Him.

He and you together will make your heart peace-filled. You must seek peace, then He will grant it. That is not to say that you will be freed from the cacophony of the world all around you, but rather that you will not be overwhelmed by the noise pollution, when the Lord is in your heart. He will provide for you a spiritual insulation that will grant you the aspects of peace that allow for the development of the other virtues that will bring you ever nearer to a true harmony with the Lord.

42
A Beautiful Thing

Jesus said to them, "Why do you trouble the woman? For she has done a beautiful thing to me." (Matthew 26:10)

He had a way of defending women against oppression by groups. Recall His conversation with the woman of Samaria who was forced to fetch her water in the mid-afternoon in order to avoid the humiliation of her fellow female villagers who would taunt her for her many infidelities. And that other woman, nameless as well, who had been taken in the act of adultery and nearly stoned to death; if it had not been for His protection, saving her life by challenging her accusers with their own hidden sins, she would have been killed.

In the case quoted above, Jesus is again defending a woman whose name we are not given. He calls attention to her kindness, since it is a labor of overwhelming love that she is performing. Jesus used the incident to suggest the mystical manner God has of working His will incognito. The woman herself was not at all aware that she had been fulfilling the will of God. Jesus points out that she was doing what was in her capacity to do—gathering up her entire savings, purchasing the most expensive vessel of perfumed ointment obtainable, then rushing to the dinner where she knew He would be present in order to anoint the One who had done more than anybody else in her life for her. She broke the costly contents above His head and let it run down upon his hair and face.

Imagine the reaction of those in attendance, especially the women who merely waited on the men from the kitchen, never daring to enter the dining area except to set out the next course or to clear the utensils. Brazen! Impertinent! Showing off! Then when the men there at table grumbled over the breach of propriety and customs, more so by a woman, Jesus spoke out in her behalf.

In the spontaneous act of love the mysterious woman with the precious ointment acted as though she were the prophet Samuel anointing the head of the future king Saul, for Jesus was in an even greater sense the ruler and king of the Jews, as Pilate would soon after make clear to the world. She was manifesting Jesus as the Christ, the word meaning the "anointed one." And how like the Lord to choose such a setting as this to manifest His special Son as His appointed One, by this seemingly accidental sign of precious oils poured out upon His head. Let those with faith comprehend the hidden meaning of His royalty, for He would shortly afterwards announce to Pilate that His Kingdom was not of this world. He was to pass through death, even invading the realm of the dead to release those held there in captivity and make a way for them to the Kingdom of Heaven.

But those who understood not a bit of this argued that she should have given her money to the poor if she really wanted to do something worthy of a blessing. The argument is a sound one, and it would be used through the centuries time and time again, against the Church of Christ. In our century, Lenin stripped the churches of their wealth by pretending to obtain for the poor and needy what Patriarch Tikhon, head of the Russian Orthodox Church, was offering of his own free will. Even in our days the essential act of caring for the needy too frequently is distorted, as though the exclusive reason for the existence of the Church is to provide social welfare.

How wise of Him to make them realize that it was not a

matter of choosing either the poor or Himself, as if the woman indeed had made a conscious choice and decided to reject the welfare of the impoverished. This was rather an instance of the priority of love. She might have contributed to the poor the cost of that expensive nard, but until that very moment of her impulsiveness she never thought of herself as wealthy. Her accusers may have had many times more the value of the perfume in their own savings, yet like the rich young man they would not consider "selling all they have and giving it to the poor." It was a commitment of love, and she loved Jesus entirely.

The lesson is for us all, for which of us has not been at times so cautious and overly prudent that we hesitated, waiting and seeing, rather than grasping the fleeting moment of life as it presented itself to us, only to spend a lifetime of regret over what decisive action we failed to take. That unknown woman possessed by a burning love for Jesus was able to seize the moment. Jesus was not with them for long. Some instinct —was it women's intuition?—compelled her to do that "beautiful thing" which nobody else even considered. Truly it was a labor of love, and as such it took precedent over any mere gift of charity, such as a contribution to the poor. More than that, she was unintentionally fulfilling the will of God by preparing Jesus for His burial. Jesus realized what His disciples would only begin to appreciate much later: He was sent to earth to accomplish a divine mission that included His own death. The love-filled woman had a role in fulfilling that sacred destiny.

43
Love and Hate: The Conflict Within

But I tell you who hear me: Love your enemies, do good to those who hate you, bless those who curse you, pray for those who mistreat you. (Luke 6:27)

To be a member of the Church is not very difficult. Normally, one is baptized into the Body of Christ as an infant. In adulthood, the requirements are usually minimal and there is no punishment, except in extreme circumstances, for failing to comply with the rules of the Church, as long as one repents and returns to the fold. But to do the will of Jesus Christ is not at all a simple matter. We ought to make this significant distinction quite clear to every "member of good standing": church membership is not at all a guarantee of a place in the Kingdom of God.

Christ's Gospel orders us to love. Those who cannot or will not, shall not become citizens of heaven. There is no place in heaven for anger, hate, revenge, cruelty, envy, or spite. This is not negotiable. If those traits, or more properly sins, are in any degree inside us, they must be removed while there remains breath in our lungs, for they align us with the enemies of Jesus Christ, and not His friends. Those passions cannot be trivialized or defended—they must be purged. Here is a vivid description of anger in control of a human being:

> It is true, I suppose, that nobody finds it exactly pleasant to be criticized or shouted at, but I see in the face of the human being raging at me a wild animal in its true colors, one more horrible than any lion. . . . Anger makes them reveal in a flash human nature in all its horror.
>
> (Dazai Osamu, "No Longer Human")

The problem for all Christians is that we now live in a pagan world which rewards and encourages aggressive behavior. Somehow we must deal with this reality. Athletics is a prime example, and so is the manner in which automobile drivers relate to one another from behind the wheel. Secular psychologists for the most part counsel their clients to release their hostilities and inner feelings of aggression, considering such release to be therapeutic. They would reject the above quotation which holds that anger reveals human nature "in all its horror." Quite the contrary, they would insist, anger is instinctive and natural.

Jesus Christ, however, makes demands on His followers which impose harsh decisions. The implication of His Gospel message is that anger is not truly natural to us except in our fallen state. Humans were created by God to love and to be loved. Those who would protest are reducing human beings to simple animals. A lion growls and prepares to kill when his territory is invaded, when he is hungry, or when he is challenged by a rival. Is it the same with a human being?

If we choose to follow Christ and to love always, never surrendering to anger or hatred, we shall require the gifts He brings us from His Father in heaven. Those gifts are called grace, and we cannot do without them. Here is what is happening when we receive Christ from the chalice: Grace is imparted to us, as it is also whenever we are united with God in our prayers or when we comprehend His Word in the sacred worship of the Church. Without grace we will be unable to resist feeling what the world terms natural emotions, but which the gospel insists are the sins that must be overcome and driven out of our personalities as we move forward in this life toward the Kingdom of God.

44
Created for Love

Therefore I tell you her many sins are forgiven—for she loved much.
(Luke 7:47)

Imagine the setting: Jesus had been invited to dinner with His disciples at the home of a Pharisee, when a woman known for her loose way of living in the community entered boldly, breaking a vial of expensive perfume at the feet of Jesus, weeping and wiping His feet with her hair. It was not her behavior that shocked them all, but His, for they all knew her reputation. They expected Him to rebuke her and send her away, but He allowed her to express herself in such an unusual manner. Nobody else understood what had happened to her, for if they had, they might have realized that God in Christ had forgiven her sins. Jesus was offering them a preview of that ultimate meeting each of us shall have with Him at the conclusion of this life on earth.

The woman comprehended from looking into His eyes not only that all of her many sins were known to Him, but that He saw in her the person God had created her to be. She who had had many partners in the love act understood that she had been created for love—but this is not the same as the satisfaction of male urges and fantasies. Rather, the love deeper and fuller than sex is a response to the Creator, a self-offering of her whole being to the One who gave her life.

Her self-realization in the eyes of Jesus was a judgment; yet it could as well be termed recognition of the person we truly were made to be. Something like this occurs when we scrutinize the ways of a person who is living a totally Christian life. Instinctively we compare ourselves to that person. We measure our own lives by her or his stature. If we have mere human models, we may discover their flaws and take pride in presuming we are not so bad after all, or if the person appears to be above reproach, we may feel inferior, envying the other and winding up with guilt over our pettiness of character.

In the case of Jesus, who is the perfect model, envy is not possible since He does not draw attention to Himself as a domineering egotist to whom all others should surrender their own identities—as is the case for so many all too human leaders. The Alexanders and Napoleons were men who led others into wars, danger, and even to their death by using their skills of persuasion and leadership, offering some cause which at least appeared to enhance the personalities of their followers, giving them something outside of themselves to live for. All too many people have a low self-image. They look upon themselves as little people without much intrinsic value. They are quite eager to offer their freedom to anybody with a dominating will, submerging their personalities in the ocean of mass appeal, eagerly devoting themselves and their wills to the will of the "Great Person" whose plan, or at least whose enormous ego, requires complete obedience from his followers.

Jesus was radically unlike any of the numerous self-promoters made famous through the course of history. His purpose was the opposite of such world leaders. They demand self-surrender, while Jesus invites self-awareness. Their call is to follow and to lose the need for self-evaluation. Jesus' message is "Follow me," and in the process, grow to realize who you truly are and were intended to become by being obedient to God's will, discovering the person the Father had in mind when He created you. The world's leaders justify all their actions, even those that should bring about their guilt, by the self-righteousness of the common cause. Jesus on the other hand confronts us with the facts of our lives and the reality of our sinfulness, not excusing or exempting our wrongdoings, but by forgiving our sins He liberates us to love purely, sincerely, and completely the Father who created us, the Son who set us free from enslavement to sin, and the Holy Spirit who prays continually that our eyes may be opened to the realization of who we are, where we have come from and where we are destined to go in order to be the person we really are to the God who made us.

45
Mystery of Gift and Giver

For God so loved the world that He gave His only Son, that whoever believes in Him should not perish but have eternal life. (John 3:16)

An old Russian parable states: "It is not the gift that is precious, it is the love." Yes, there is truth in that statement, for we do look beyond the gift and appreciate the intention of the giver. Actually, Russians and Americans have somewhat different customs in gift giving. An American will usually not present something to another person without first having it elaborately gift-wrapped. Notice, for example, the presents under the tree on Christmas morning. The package is almost as important as its contents. But a Russian offers without ostentation, and frequently does so in a casual manner. The present may be in a plain brown paper wrapping or not covered at all. He simply wants the other to have some part of himself.

For the God we know in the sacred Scriptures and Holy Church, both gift and giver transcend any meaning we can readily fathom. The precious gift of God is Christ Jesus, and the love that comes in Him is of the Father. Who can claim to comprehend that holy mystery?

What a gift is Christ, and how unworthy is the world to receive Him. Do you recall the photograph, actually the negative, of the famous Shroud of Turin, with what just might be the very image of Jesus emblazoned upon it? The battered face, the smashed nose, the streaks of blood that transpose as illumination on the film—all are witness to the brutal, savage treatment of God's precious gift. Why? What caused them to hate Him so? And why, even today, must some true believers suffer for their unstinting love of Him in the Gulag prisons of the Soviet Union? Ignorance might be pardoned—an infant, say, who had captured a butterfly only to tear it apart in order to learn what it's made of, or even adults who cannot comprehend what they are doing with bulldozers when they destroy virgin forests to make a road for "progress."

When we Christians announce love as a mighty mystery, we are signifying our helplessness in trying to learn about God's love. There is no rational answer to the query: Why does He love us so? Nothing we have achieved merits it. Some claim that God's justice, or righteousness, demands that what He created be restored to its original form in order that the Creator not be humiliated by a shabby product. Parts of the Old Testament—for example, Amos—favor that understanding of redemption. Still, there is more. That legalistic explanation does not embrace the dimensions of love.

He loved the world so much that He offered the most precious object of His love for the sake of the world. We might wonder who of us, in the world and part of it, love the world in equal measure? How can we begin to grasp the import of what is taking place in the coming of Christ?

When an Orthodox Christian gazes at the icon of the infant Jesus in the arms of His mother, he sees God's child there, held by her. He is the only real gift of Christmas. He is evidence of God's love for the world.

And she, His mother—what does she understand of that love of the Father for the world? The difficulty, the "problem" of the iconographer, is to elucidate the degree of the holy lady's grasp of the mystery of divine love which is made manifest in her arms. The comprehension will grow and develop in her through the years of infancy until the time she will stand at the base of His cross. She must have had a presentiment of what would be, some insight as to what was the meaning and purpose of His sacred life here on earth. How is that revealed in an icon? By our own meditations on her experiences we may grow in our insights into the significance of that precious gift, and the intention of the Giver.

46
Circle of Love

Jesus knew that the time had come for Him to leave the world and to go to the Father. Having loved His own who were in the world, He loved them to the end. (John 13:1)

Without fail somebody at the reception following an Orthodox wedding will inquire about the meaning of the procession, three times making a circle around the table in the center of the Church, the movement that highlights and climaxes the mystery of marriage. Even our own young people are so conditioned to conventional western marriages with a processional and a recessional, between which the couple "exchanges vows," that they fail to recognize the self-evident statement made in the movement around the table that holds the holy Gospel. They go forth, bound to one another, bearing flames of light ("while you have the light, walk in the light," Jn 12:35), wearing the crowns adorning those who are called to wear crowns in God's Kingdom; and they follow the Cross of Christ. How can it be that such obvious symbols require elucidation?

Whatever else may require an explanation, let the newlyweds at least realize the fundamental reality: Christ is ahead of them as well as within their lives to the extent that they will open their hearts to receive Him. Not for a while, but forever, as in the verse above, "He loved them to the end."

Here is the symbol of the circle, illustrated for those requiring elucidation. To those persons fixated on this world only, "going in circles" signifies having lost one's direction. For those attuned to the ways of the Spirit, however, the circle reminds them of their place won in eternity by Jesus Christ. As John Donne wrote:

> One of the most convenient Hieroglyphicks of God is a Circle; and a Circle is endlesse: whom God loves, hee loves to the end: and not onley to their death, but to his end, and his end is, that he might love them still. (from *Donne's Sermons*)

The key to comprehending the meaning of Christ's love lies in the tiny words within the verse above: "His own." The Lord's love, St John reminds us, is not indiscriminate. The object of His love is "His own." Love is personal, from one living being to another. Think of the popular T-shirts that point to the partner, so that the world may know one belongs to the other.

You, when you make the sign of the cross on yourself, are announcing that you belong to Christ. You are one of "His own." Many make an obsession of becoming a member in some fraternity or sorority, a school group or a select organization. They feel they can only prove their worth to themselves if they are admitted to a certain college, if they are chosen for the team or cheerleading squad, perhaps the band or orchestra, or the post for which they had been interviewed. What does that say about the inner security, not to mention the emotional stability, of such persons who must have a steady stream of reassurances from outside themselves to prove they are wanted, needed, worthy, important, lovely, and acceptable in the groups that comprise society?

All of those groups, organizations, and cliques are of far less importance than realizing that one is included among the ranks of "His own," those who are invited to sit at table with the apostles and saints of every generation, those who have given themselves over to Christ's everlasting love.

And He loves His own "to the end." What happiness is expressed in that touch of irony, for we must realize that there is not an end for the Lord. What we call the end of life is only the start of the state of existence in that reality called the Kingdom of God. This world's sunset is followed not by night, but by the bright light of a new day with God in Christ. John Donne was one of the world's greatest poets, a person who enjoyed a play on words such as "end." For him it had two meanings: a terminal point and a purpose. He is playing a delightful trick, for he pretends to suggest that Christ's love lasts to the final moment, but the discerning reader realizes that he means that instead it is Christ's purpose to love us through death, to warm our corpses with the heat of His love, to embrace our limp, dead weight, keeping us from falling into the abyss, lifting us, bearing us through the dark night of death to the eternal sunrise of His Father's realm. All that is to be brought about by supernal love. This, then, is the embrace of Christ.

47
The Father's Love

If a person loves me he will keep my word, and my Father will love him, and we will come to him and make our home with him. (John 14:22)

We may acknowledge the insight of Sigmund Freud regarding the relationships among the members of a family marked by the famous Oedipus complex. It helps explain why sometimes boys have difficulty relating to their fathers, but the insight is not universally applicable and should be tested against Christian family values.

Freud utilized the ancient myth of Oedipus, who killed his father and married his mother, only to blind himself when he discovered he had done so, as an explanation of a universal reality of family relationships, that in every family the male child will desire instinctively to replace his father in the affections of his mother. Realizing this to be wrong, evil, and impossible, the male child feels guilt and the fear of punishment by his father, punishment in the form of castration. Freud recognized in himself an inordinate desire for his mother, and he owned up to despising his father for a supposed weakness of character. But to project such a relationship into every child-parent relationship is excessive. That he was successful in convincing western civilization that such is the case is a tribute to Freud's power of persuasion, as well as to the suggestibility of humankind.

How better to corrode the sacred bond of parent and child than to suggest to the world that incest is the natural urge of every male infant? Is it not interesting that a culture priding itself on scientific objectivity would assume without challenge that the competition between an infant son and his father for the affection of the mother is basic to each family relationship? Christians more than others should reject that credo of psychoanalysis not only because of the destruction it causes to the core of the family, but because our theology is based on the love between the heavenly Father and Son, the everlasting Creator God and His Word who had been incarnated into our world and revealed to us in Jesus Christ.

And what does Jesus teach about that relationship but that it is permeated and circumscribed with selfless love. Can anybody read the Gospels and not be made aware of the emphasis on love that Jesus constantly manifests and calls for? The response of Jesus to His Father's love is apparent in His cross. Beyond mere reason Jesus proved His devotion to His Father's will by enduring to the end all that the crucifixion imposed on Him.

That love between the heavenly Father and Jesus which the Savior invites us to share in the keeping of His Word—that very love relationship has to be the model for our human father-son relationships, as well. Let us put behind the myth of Oedipus, or at least reject the application of that Greek fable as offered by Freud, when we are involved with our own family's interpersonal dynamics. Orthodox Christians especially, who are ever gazing at the various icons of the Theotokos and the Christ child, have more cause than other Christians to refute the ideas that Freudians have perpetrated on western culture. Here is evidence of what we would term a normal, spiritual affection between son and mother—could that possibly be construed as other than holy, pure, and innocent? But Freud's concept of love was what we would call lust, that is, passion that excludes other persons, including a father, an obsessive attachment demanding all attention for oneself. And it is not only for the unique relationship shared between Christ and His blessed mother. Read this evidence of what we would interpret to be the normal affection of a son for his father:

> I am amazed how much my father and mother have given me and how their quiet life goes on in me, albeit indirectly. How vivid in my memory are all those places . . . where they lived before I was born—I have never been there and it makes no sense, but I can't get them out of my mind. I recall my father's snoring as something protective. Hearing it I felt safe. And his smell was protection too.
>
> (Abram Tertz, pen name of Andrei Sinyavsky, *A Voice from the Chorus*, p. 231)

Here we have a man in his mid-forties, imprisoned in the infamous Gulag penal system of the USSR, who is reflecting on the shared joy of his early years with his parents. His father, even asleep, afforded him the assurance of his protection. His snoring was a sign of peace and safety, in a home where the father was able to rest easily.

Notice, also, the mention of his father's smell. Is this natural? Certainly more so than the Freudian insistence on a competition between father and son over the affection of the mother, with the resulting guilt. So natural is this scent that we need only observe male beasts in the forests and jungles who purposely exude a scent of their musk on their territorial rocks and trees, announcing their presence so that the aroma will be taken as a warning to strangers, and to their own offspring, as a sign of their protection.

Notice how simply the Savior in the quotation above assumes that His Father will love those whom Jesus loves. Such a presumption could flow only from a confidence based on a total love relationship. The Father would never disappoint the Son, and the Son can trust implicitly the Father's loving care. We should imitate such mutual reliance even though we are mere human beings, because we are baptized into Christ and should be growing ever more in the knowledge of Him; therefore, we have an example in Him, and we comprehend the affection of the God who reveals Himself as perfect Father, whose ideal Son is Jesus Christ, the same God who has adopted us into His sacred family.

48
Two Kinds of Love

Near the cross of Jesus stood his mother and his mother's sister, Mary the wife of Clopas, and Mary of Magdala. Seeing his mother and the disciple he loved standing near her, Jesus said to his mother, "Woman, this is your son." Then to the disciple he said, "This is your mother." And from that moment the disciple made a place for her in his home.
(John 19:25)

What does a man who has nothing at all in material wealth leave for his legacy? How does one draw up and execute a last will and testament when his very clothing had been taken from his body to be apportioned to pay for the cost of his execution?

Our Lord who had nowhere to lay His head had nothing to leave but love and an immense treasury of memories stored in the hearts and minds of those He loved most. That wealth He distributed from the cross to those He knew were sure to value it the highest.

There are two kinds of love, general and specific. Most of us choose one or the other, but Jesus Christ achieved both. To love mankind in general is partial and deluded. The one who came as the Savior of the world, the Savior of everybody of every race and language including all those living, the ones already dead, and the billions yet to be born, is capable of loving and saving all people because He is able to love specific persons. More than anybody on earth, He loved His own mother and the disciple who went to be with Him at the cross and who was to wear as a mark of distinction the awareness that he was one specially loved by Jesus.

We know of world figures who gave themselves for their nation, great statesmen who are remembered with affection from one generation to another, yet whose families' lives were sacrificed in the process. King David of Israel was like that. More modern men, whom for the sake of delicacy we hesitate to mention, could care for the multitudes, yet ignore those who sit at table with them, the inheritors of their blood lines and genetic traits.

The other, more common phenomenon is with those like most of us who love our spouses, our children, and our parents, but fix there the boundary of our immediate concern. We build a fence between "mine" and "other." We are incapable, one might presume, of sacrificing beyond the immediate and personal. Our ability to feel true compassion and remorse is stunted; in fact, we often feel challenged and become hostile when a demand is placed upon us to care in an intense manner for those beyond our family. That attitude we often wrongly brand natural.

Christ was concerned both for mankind in general and for the individual who lived and suffered all around Him. From the cross He looked first into heaven to ask the forgiveness of the Father, upon all who in their ignorance oppress both Himself and all others everywhere. Perhaps we need not include the term "both," since in the Last Judgment story in Matthew 25 we learn of His unity with all of suffering humanity.

Then He looked nearby Him at His own mother and at the apostle He loved more than others, giving them His love, the only gift He had—the love of that most special son for His mother, the love He had for the only apostle willing at that moment to risk his own life just to be with his dying leader.

Love unites; therefore let them be united. Love relates one to another, so let them be now bound into a relationship which transcends the closest family ties. Let them become by their love the first members of the family of God.

49
Do You Love Me?

He said to him a third time, "Simon, son of John, do you love me?" Peter was grieved because he said to him the third time, "Do you love me?" And he said to him, "Lord, you know everything; you know that I love you."
(John 21:17)

St John the Evangelist surely must have had a sense of humor to record the conversation between the resurrected Lord Jesus and Peter, at the close of his Gospel and just before Christ was to ascend to the Kingdom of Heaven. Humorous is St Peter's exasperation in being asked three times of his love for Jesus. "You know everything," he granted with indignation, yet it was only a brief time after the day of the crucifixion when the one who knows everything predicted he would deny him thrice. Then, also, Peter contradicted the Lord, only to act out the prophecy.

In a tender scenario identifiable to anybody with parents or grandparents from the Old World, Tevye in a scene from the musical *Fiddler on the Roof* gathers up his courage and asks his wife point blank, "Do you lahv me?" She, indignant and confused at such an odd question, proceeds to list *seriatim* all the proofs of her love by her actions on his behalf for the past quarter century: "I wash your clothes, I mend your shirts, I cook your food, I . . ."

Yes, he acknowledges all of that, but . . . "Do you *lahv*

me?" he persists. Need she put into words what her whole being had been communicating all those years? What more does he expect from her? Is he really so insensitive to her affections, or does Tevye comprehend that one can love and obey a spouse, even share all the joys and sorrows of married life, yet do it all as a duty, not necessarily from a deep feeling of love. Love must be expressed, and he is properly insisting on her communicating her affection, even as difficult as it is for her to do so.

You know those who argue that God, who knows everything, realizes they love Him, and so there is no real need for daily prayers or regular church attendance, but Tevye's logic holds. If you love the Lord you must tell Him so, not for His sake, but because we ourselves require reminders of our values, the chief of them being the love of the Lord. It is we who are fickle, capable of deceiving our minds into making empty confessions of God's love, while we spend our time almost exclusively devoted to ourselves.

Love is total commitment, and if it is not that, then we are using the incorrect term. We today abuse language so much that we claim to "love," at least on TV commercials, soap and salad dressings; however, Christians are by definition committed persons, devoted to God, measuring all of their relationships by the love they have for the Holy Trinity.

One deeper aspect of Christ's insistence on Peter's threefold profession of his love was to eradicate by each avowal of his love one of his earlier denials of Christ. What indeed have we to offer Him except our love. Since we have no defense for the innumerable sins committed against God, we can at least have an abiding love for Him. Even the term love, when we say it, comes out with a hollow, sometimes fickle, even dull echo, because we are as inconsistent as the apostle that Jesus named the "Rock"; yet the Lord God is overwhelming in His mercy. He will accept our love just as we present it, in order that we may grow in the ability to love more purely, clearly, and consistently.

50
Loving Oneself the Right Way

In all this, remember how critical the moment is. It is time for you to wake out of sleep, for deliverance is nearer to us now than it was when first we believed. It is far on in the night; day is near. Let us therefore throw off the deeds of darkness and put on our armor as soldiers of the light. Let us behave with decency as befits the day; no reveling or drunkenness, no gluttony or lewdness, no quarrels or jealousies! Let Christ Jesus himself be the armor you wear; give no more thought to satisfying the bodily appetite.
(Romans 13:11-14)

Approximately half of the year's days are given to fasting in the calendar of the Orthodox Church, and the most intensive period of fasting and self-mortification is during the pre-paschal time. Silence is the only appropriate reply to those who say, "What purpose is there to the proscriptions and restrictions imposed upon us modern Christians by the Church during Great Lent?" The response would need to take into account the presumption that there is such an entity as the modern Christian who is so different from all the Church's predecessors in the faith that the rules and spiritual discipline traditional throughout the history of Orthodoxy are no longer applicable.

The modern man, as we are led to believe from our contemporary literature, is a creature possessing total freedom without responsibility to anybody for his life and actions, neither to God nor to his parents, much less to his spouse, his neighbor, or to society in general. Nothing may stand in the way to his happiness. If marriage becomes burdensome, file for a divorce. If parents annoy him, leave home immediately and forget them. In every way possible, always enjoy yourself, and if something unpleasant gets in the way, then shove it aside, abort it, or run away from it. Here in a capsule is the philosophy of the modern hedonistic person.

To a person with such a mind-set Lent would be more than burdensome; it would be ridiculous, even offensive. Self-gratification is the only reason for living, and nothing is too good for him. The greatest tragedy would be to die without having exhausted himself in gratifying his senses and imagination in all the pleasures this world provides. The only concept of sacrament is experience, of every type and intensity. How dare we suggest that he deprive himself of forty springtime days and nights of delight.

Lent is only for those who truly desire to become part of something greater than they, experiencing a joy transcending mere titillation of the five senses. Lent includes sacrificing one's whole life and will, not just food and entertainment. It is the commitment of one's being to a reality far more meaningful than any sensual pleasure of the moment. It is a call to share in the very source of life itself.

Here is a discipline for those willing to accept it, as a means by which they come to know themselves more fully, discovering the extent to which they have relied upon material objects for pleasure and diversion, perceiving how the selling of themselves for mere inanimate objects or to those who flatter them and promise the good life has made them less than whole, noble, integral, and pure, free and precious in the sight of God. Lent reveals to us what has happened on the way to salvation that has prevented us from reaching the unity with God which is the only real purpose for living;

then we may take the route back to Him again, restoring within us the image in which we were fashioned. Here is a way not for the hedonist or the spiritually blind, but for those who are in search of their true selves.

51
Awareness of God's Love

For we are the temple of the living God. As God has said: "I will live with them and walk among them, and I will be their God and they will be my people."
(2 Corinthians 6:16)

To grow in the love of God is to become ever more consciously aware of what He wants of us, and primarily that is to become united unreservedly, totally, and consciously with the Holy Trinity. How foolish we are if we should imagine that faith in God can be utilitarian, that is, that we can utilize the love that the Lord has for us in order to achieve our own purposes on earth, as though He were like a powerful, wealthy relative whose favor we curry to gain advantage for ourselves.

Note the bold metaphor St Paul uses: "We are the temple of the living God." He intends it not as hyperbole, as exaggerated poetic expression designed to capture the imagination of his readers, but as a logical conclusion to what appears in the Old Testament at several places. In the Torah, Leviticus 26:12, the same desire of the Lord is mentioned. It later is recalled by the prophets, in Jeremiah 32:38 and Ezekiel 37:27.

For us it is important to realize that we *already* are the temple, not merely that we shall become so one day or that at some point in history we were the temple of the living God. Indeed, we are the place where the Lord has taken up an abode, from the moment we were baptized into Christ and, as the processional hymn from St Paul's epistles affirms, "have put on Christ." From that moment we are called to grow ever more aware of the unity with the Holy Trinity that is the Lord's plan for us. In order to do so, however, it is imperative that we struggle with sin, for evil is completely alien to God. Also, we must develop the knowledge that it is truly God who abides within us. Sin prevents that consciousness from taking place by obscuring the inner vision of that unity.

St Symeon the New Theologian wrote of the necessity to be aware of the presence of the Almighty within us through grace. In his vivid image, just as no pregnant woman could be incapable of realizing and experiencing the living being within her womb, so we should also strive to recognize the Lord who dwells within us. Perhaps one might counter that faith is sufficient and the passionate urge to know the God within might be considered a lack of faith, but such a faith would be passive, a basic lack of desire to grow into unity with the One who chooses to abide within us and to fill us with Himself.

> And how is it that one made god by grace and by adoption will not be god in awareness and knowledge and contemplation, he who has put on the Son of God? (St Symeon, Hymn 50)

The United States Army, in its appeal to enlist the young people of this nation into its services, has adopted the slogan: "Be all that you can be." We might borrow that phrase, which offers quite sound advice. Beyond what the Army's slogan suggests, more than a career or job training, more than having a secure future, wealth, fame, a position of authority or the benefits of what this world sets forth as the good life, one can become wholly the person whom God had created. Everything that one can be is not even revealed to us in this life, since this world obscures what God had intended for us.

Our insight is opaque because of the world. The implications of original sin include the fact that we are not capable of normally realizing the potential latent within our selves. By grace, the Lord is constantly reaching out to us, offering every opportunity to grow in the only sure and total manner possible, by developing the awareness of His presence within, and building upon that relationship with the sacred Trinity with all our heart, soul, body, and mind.

52
Christians Know How to Love

It is right for me to feel this way about all of you, since I have you in my heart. (Philippians 1:7)

What a wonderful phrase to express one's feelings for others: "I have you in my heart." Our society talks, sings, writes, and shouts about love and lovers without realizing that to do so lightly makes such a beautiful emotion ordinary almost to meaninglessness, fit for jingles and bumper stickers. If Christians will take up the holy task of redeeming love's purity and wholesomeness, what better way to begin than to contemplate the winsome phrase of St Paul: "I have you in my heart."

We often say to one another, "I had you on my mind," which is itself a compliment, especially in a culture that encourages individualism and expects us to be preoccupied with ourselves and our personal problems. To have someone in mind implies at least that we thought about them. Perhaps a word we had heard or a place we had visited reminded us of the one who bubbled up into the mind's consciousness, jarring to the surface the memory of a similar time since past that had been shared with the one in mind. We claim to forget place, persons, and events, but the mind never truly forgets. It merely files away for future reference the signals and messages that would only clutter the consciousness and cause it to malfunction. We cannot have all the people of our past constantly before us, or we would jam the circuits of our mind by what we term obsessions.

Yet, can we truly have a multitude of persons in our hearts? I believe so. The heart is the core of our emotions, and emotions are not as logical as thoughts. Emotions are affected by others who by loving us and caring for us warm our inner beings with their glowing presence. We draw strength from those who love us. That love is not insignificant sentimentality, but warmth and light, radiating within our hearts when an adverse circumstance surrounds us with cold, dark, negative feelings. And the ones in our hearts can warm our hearts even from the grave, but better put, from the life they live in the Kingdom beyond the earth.

How much more love we share with those in our hearts than we could gain from mere sexual relations. How pathetically inadequate it is to reduce love to mere sexuality, when the love experienced by those who have in their hearts the Spirit of Christ radiates through a mystical network all the positive emotions proceeding from the Holy Trinity. Sexual love is exclusive of all but the couple engaged in the act, but spiritual love includes all who consciously affirm the love of God in Christ Jesus as experienced by those He loves who share in that love by loving one another.

53
Who Teaches Love and Kindness?

I am reminded of the sincerity of your faith, a faith which was alive in Lois your grandmother and Eunice your mother before you, and which, I am confident, lives in you also.
(2 Timothy 1:5)

St Paul in writing to his young disciple, Timothy, counsels him as a father would, reaffirming the faith he knows is deep inside him, even though the youth may not have the firmness of will and strength of character which the holy apostle himself possessed. Apparently word had come to the older man of a setback in Timothy's life, a failure of nerve that almost all of us experience at some time or another in a lifetime.

Maybe in reflecting upon young Timothy, St Paul was wondering about the way he might bring out the leadership qualities needed to make him an inspired apostle of Christ in that time of extreme turbulence in the small Christian community. After meditation, he affirmed that Timothy would come out of it all right, if for no other reason than that he had strong spiritual roots. Both his grandmother and mother were so firmly grounded in the Lord that surely he must have inherited something of their moral fiber and unshakable faith.

Does this not speak a word to the culture of today? Here

is a case in which women obviously have taken a leadership role in their household, for St Paul presumes and relies upon their having had the ability to influence the men in their homes.

So much is right and just in the movement today for women's rights. They ought to have equal employment opportunities, equal wages for similar job descriptions, and many more social and political benefits and fair treatment, but all of that ought not to be at the expense of the family. Christians will not long accept any weakening of the family unit or the overthrow of the traditional role of the mother in the home, and her duty to raise and influence her children. Whenever the marriage bonds are being weakened and the family unity is in jeopardy, when society decides to encourage weakening of the parent-child relationship, eventually the Church will address the situation. In the subtle balance of values, ways must be set forth for lifting up the real need to elevate the status and dignity of women in society without in the process jeopardizing the family unit.

Surely society has been negligent in opening roles for women in the institutions of culture. At the same time, the Church must do all in its power to grant dignity to the woman's role in the family. We must do all in our power to raise up from the young women in our spiritual communities new generations of Loises and Eunices who will love and undertake to learn about their faith and the values proceeding from it, treasuring it as their most precious heritage, inculcating it into the offspring entrusted to them by the Lord. The dignity of woman in the secular world must not come at the expense of the dignity of homemakers and mothers. To them is entrusted the care and the responsibility for teaching true values to those of their wombs. Who else will teach children the need to submit their selfish demands and cravings to the greater welfare of the whole community? Where will young people learn that self-gratification is not the highest purpose of this life on earth. How will they learn kindness, self-sacrifice, respect, humility, finding a joy in those virtues? The strength and effectiveness of our Churches is in direct relation to the zeal and health of our families. Truly the home is a chapel where the people of Christ abide. We cannot do enough to uphold the dignity and self-worth of those who abide there; our greatest assets are the mothers in our homes.

54
God is Love

God is Love. (1 John 4:8)

The renowned, yet deceptively simple sentence that appears to identify God with the quality of love appears in the first epistle of John. Deceptive, because it requires more than a mite of explanation to clarify what is meant. In fact it would serve as a case in point to lift up the need for instruction by the Church, for those who follow the fallacy of fundamentalism insist that the sacred scriptures are self-explanatory, requiring little explanation to be comprehended completely.

The greatest novelist and one might say genius, Leo Tolstoy, put aside the Orthodox Christian faith into which he had been baptized, insisting that it was an impediment to his spiritual progress. In his classic novel, *War and Peace,* he interpreted this famous Johannine passage:

> Love is God, and to die means that I, a particle of love, shall return to the general and eternal source. (VII,6)

Such an idea is purely pagan, though its sentiment is rather positive. It reflects the mentality of primitive religions both Hellenic and Oriental, and its antecedents are not difficult to discover. Tolstoy was like so many today who after leaving the Church presume that being outside provides them a vantage point that enables them to see even better the essentials of faith, because they can be more objective than believers. The faithful, on the other hand, might consider them like children on the sidewalk outside a bakery shop who peer in at the cakes in the display case. In a sense they are able to describe the appearance, but if they cannot read the writing on the surface, much less smell or taste them, not to speak of knowing the purpose of the cakes—birthday party, wedding, anniversary—how much do they really know about them?

Again, in the phrase "God is love" we might add that Tolstoy's definition is incorrect simply because it is limited. Love is not a cosmic, invisible essence, part of which inhabits our souls. Rather, love is always related to the persons who receive its meaning, who discover love in the process of their relationships.

God is a person, and He relates to us in a personal way. This is a wonderous insight, for in it we can be assured that love is not obscure or completely incomprehensible, not even that kind which some parents call love when they claim to love their children, yet deal with them in ways that are contrary to true love. The love of one person for another is readily understood, and by both parties. More than a state of being, it always makes itself evident to the other. God is not merely letting us know He loves us through the words of the Bible; He is demonstrating that affection in our lives and in the world. We only have to learn how to look for it.

The apostles, for instance, were pointing to God's love for the world when they proclaimed that love in Jesus Christ. He is the evidence. To those who knew the Bible, they would explain the predictions of what God achieved in Christ by the anticipations of Christ in the history of the Hebrew people. For those who were ignorant of the Bible, they utilized the evidence of God's workings in nature, in order to show His love for all creation by the way He brought forth the best in all that exists. In all cases, they make the presumption that any human being with an average intelligence is capable of understanding that God is the cause of the universe, which is not a mere accident, and that God is not hiding His actions from His creatures. All He does is positive, in the final analysis, because His desire is for the welfare of all that He has created. He deals with everything kindly and justly; however, in His relationship with the highest form of creatures, the human being, He decided to base the relationship on love. And He is still reaching out to us with love if we choose to accept it. That wonderful mystery lies at the root of the union in Him that God is extending to each one of us. Praise be to His Holy Name.

55
You are Loved

In this is love; not that we loved God, but that He loved us.
(1 John 4:10)

London's Foundling Hospital had a mysterious problem. None of the physicians were able to explain why some of the infants kept on living while others—in fact the majority—were so suddenly dying. The babies were monitored closely, the staff were all queried, and the medicines were scrutinized. All that anybody came up with was that the children on the floor where the chores were done by Annie, an old cleaning woman, were the ones who lived. Annie was watched without her knowing. What she did was so natural that it went without notice at first, but after her tasks of dusting and mopping, she would hold each baby for a while and sing to it. That's all—but it made a life or death difference.

Psychologists today speak of subliminal suggestions as though they had invented the concept. Experiments are performed by writing "popcorn," for instance, on certain frames of the films run at a theater, then noting whether viewers purchase more than the usual amount of popcorn. Of course they do. We are creatures of suggestion.

No Eastern Church exists without an icon of the Holy Theotokos and ever virgin Mary holding her infant son, our Savior Jesus Christ. Here, also, is the power of suggestion, for the one who stands in church, consciously aware of it or not, is being reminded of love. How better could the Church possibly explain God's love for the world? Whatever does it signify? Would it help our understanding if we should begin with the love we had first experienced at birth, and probably even while we were within our mothers' wombs? How more effectively could love be exemplified than by recalling our first awareness of being cared for, held in gentle hands and touched with affection, nursed and sung to by our own mothers.

Every child is precious to his own mother. Would it mean anything to a mother to remind her that there are more than six billion persons on this planet, each one having been born in circumstances similar to those of her own baby? To her, the child held in her arms is unlike any other that has ever been born, or that ever shall be. And she is right. Only to strangers are all babies alike. To the disinterested, children are a category.

But to the heavenly Father each of His children is more valuable than the child is to his own mother. That great, spiritual truth evolves within us with the growing awareness that God loves not only mankind in general, not His creation collectively, not the human race, but each one of us, as though He had made only one of us.

Would it offend any mother to be told that she could never be capable of loving her child the way God can? If so, she knows neither the Lord nor herself. All of our love is conditioned. We wish for our children that they be good, based upon what we understand goodness to be. Sometimes we cannot let go of them when it is time for the child to be free to choose, even if it means granting them the possibility of failing in the process of learning. We would hold onto them, making their decisions for them, and thus prolong their childhood. God, however, can let go, and He did so. Adam is proof of that. But Adam is also the example of how far God will go to return His creature to Himself. Christ is the proof of that.

To teach the lesson of God's love for us, we begin with Mary and the Christ child; then we complete the lesson by revealing the crucifixion of the only truly unique "child" who ever existed, and summarize by showing the icon of the resurrection in which God in Christ descends to hell in order to bring back Adam and Eve. Here indeed is love set forth.

56
Ordered to Love

Not as though I were writing you a new commandment, but the one we have had from the beginning, that we love one another.
(2 John 5:5)

After all, who nowadays obeys commands? Are we not liberated, free to do as we please? Or are we the sort of people who "keep the commandment unstained and free from reproach until the appearing of our Lord Jesus Christ" (1 Tm 6:14)? A dilemma confronts the modern Christian—if indeed this is not a contradiction in terms, for if to be modern means to be answerable to nobody, what does it mean when we call ourselves followers of Christ, or even like St Paul, slaves of Christ (Ph 1:1)? Jesus Himself said, "Why do you call me Lord, if you do not do what I command you?" (Lk 6:46). A good question. Can a Christian do as he pleases, or is he not a person under orders?

The centurion (Mt 8:5) was not a Christian, yet he saw in Jesus somebody who had at His command armies of spiritual beings ready to obey Him. Today we have people who go by the name "Christian" who resent the idea of taking orders from anybody, including the gospel and the Church of Christ. For example, the commandment to love another seems to work without much strain in a normal family setting. People who choose to live together would be naturally affectionate; however, when some element enters to disrupt the harmony even between husband and wife, a couple who elected to become united to one another forever, Christ's commandment can be overruled.

This is the weakness in this generation: Christ is not in command. The whim of the individual is the absolute authority. How fragile our bonds of union must be when they are held together by arbitrariness and whim. Nothing but individual fancy is accepted as supreme. Reason itself has fallen by the wayside—not that it had been killed, it has merely died of atrophy. We have in modern times "no-fault" divorces, which means that no reason is needed to divide a family any more, only the caprice of our partner.

Is it not amazing, this culture we live in, with its "no-fault" divorces and "no-fault" automobile insurance, suggesting a do-as-you-please lifestyle that never requires an explanation? What shall we make of the petition in every Orthodox prayer service that implores from God "A good defense before the dread judgment seat of Christ"? Term it obsolete, a vestige of another day when people feared for their place in heaven, assuming that the sacred scriptures are to be taken literally when they speak of heaven, hell, and a final judgment based on our deeds and misdeeds here on earth. What defense shall we give when called upon to account for our lives? Perhaps we ought to shop around for a faith that condones everything a person does, where worship is not so much praise to the Lord as a form of testimonial to good people who come together once a week to celebrate their goodness.

Maybe we might plead innocent by reason of insanity, basing our case on the evidence that the last decades of the twentieth century were dominated by the conviction that this generation believed itself exempt from the rules of right and wrong that had been the governing dynamic of every preceding generation. We might say that we were a people above laws and discipline, taught even in our schools that we can do as we please as long as we are "sincere" and "true to ourselves." Will that hold, I wonder, in the ultimate Supreme Court?

Not likely. From the evidence of the Gospels we must believe instead that on that day Christ Jesus, with all due tenderness and compassion, will listen carefully to such arguments, and then declare: "You know better than that. Surely you understand at the center of your heart that my love is more than merely self-love. My command was not to love yourself, but to 'love one another.' That you failed to do in your sufficient time on earth. Punish you? No, I have no intention of inflicting any punishment upon you. . . . It is enough punishment to leave you to the self you love so much. Go now. Love yourself for all eternity. That is the punishment and the 'reward' you have earned."

57
The Invitation

The Spirit and the Bride say, "Come!" And let him who hears say, "Come!" Whoever is thirsty, let him come; and whoever wishes, let him take the free gift of the water of life.
(Revelation 22:17)

How glorious and radiant a way to bring the Bible to a close. We are being invited to be with God and those in His holy Kingdom. The invitation is pronounced first from the Holy Spirit, that very Spirit who in the first words of the Bible is silently hovering over the face of the waters of creation. That quiet Spirit now sounds the initial welcome: "Come!"

The Bride of that same Spirit of the Lord who gave birth in silence to the blessed Savior, she who quietly listened to the glorious prophecy of the aged Simeon in the Temple of Jerusalem, who silently left with her appointed spouse, Joseph, for Egypt to flee the wrath of Herod, storing all those events in her heart; that mother who wept in silence as her son was being crucified and who sat demurely among the apostles on the great and holy day of Pentecost, when they were endowed with gifts of speaking in a variety of languages for the whole world to understand—that holy lady, the ever virgin Mary now utters the same invitation: "Come!"

How different the directive from the beginning of the Bible, where the heavenly Father commands Adam and Eve: "Go!" Due to their disobedience, they had been expelled from Paradise. Now, at the conclusion of the Bible the Spirit of God and the bride are inviting Adam's offspring to come and drink from the fountain of everlasting life.

Who else is extending the radiant invitation? "Let him who hears, say: 'Come!' " Does this mean everybody, altogether? Not necessarily. Jesus once spoke of those with "ears to hear, yet do not listen" (Mt 11:5). Many are they who are not open to the invitation because they are not attuned to things that are spiritual. Put another way, they are not thirsty for the righteousness that God alone provides. Let this be a lesson to us as well. How can we block out the noise of this world in order to hear the heavenly invitation?

When we are invited, we must rise quickly in response. A danger confronts modern people unlike any previous challenge: to assume that we can respond without rising and moving forward. We so comfortably and naturally sit before the television, presuming that merely by watching we are taking part in the proceedings of life, expecting that no demands are being made upon us. But the way to the Lord is through personal effort. Nobody can do it for us, just as nobody can walk on our two legs.

Finally, we have here the most positive way to look upon our own death, as well as that of those whom we love dearly in this world. If we read this joyous invitation enough times to commit it to memory, we may be spared the foolish, hopeless, unchristian temptation to tremble in despair when death comes to us. If we are able to hear the Holy Spirit and visualize the blessed mother of Christ reaching out a hand to us, inviting us to be among those who have earned a place in God's Kingdom by holding fast to the faith, despite all the adversities this world puts to us, we shall respond eagerly to that blessed invitation. How can it be that we should not take the hand of the blessed mother in heaven when she reaches out to grasp our own? "Come!" she is saying, and all those citizens of the Lord's Kingdom shall repeat the invitation. Shall we refuse?